Dear Erv and Nancy,

Thank you for being so willing to help me out all the time. A ride with you is much more fun than taking a bus!!

Love you,
Lorraine
8/03

"Leax models a wonderfully respectful approach to God's handi-work. And following the author's steps back into creation, we find both our minds and our hearts renewed. *Out Walking* is a generous, spirited offering."

—Gordon Aeschliman, president, Target Earth International

"This book presents a charming and sometimes disturbing view. Through a perceptive poet's eyes, we are given insights concerning our relationship to the shrinking natural world and are drawn to sense the presence and concern of its Author."

—J. Keith Miller, author,
The Taste of New Wine and *The Secret Life of the Soul*

"Like a hike with a good friend, this book will lead you into the splendor of the Creator's world. I enjoyed Leax's honest stories and his creative witness to the world around us."

—Stan L. LeQuire, former director,
Evangelical Environmental Network

"I greatly enjoyed walking with Leax through these stories. As I read, Leax prompted me to see through his eyes. I often sat, pages left open, brought to reflection on my own similar experiences, directed by his transparency and intrigued to follow his conclusions and insight. Such prompting helps us cherish Christ's numerous gifts and gently calls us to a life of sensitivity to God's creation."

—Mark Lassiter, director,
Christian Environmental Studies Center at Montreat College

out walking

Other Books by John Leax

Poetry

Reaching into Silence

The Task of Adam

Country Labors

Fiction

Nightwatch

Prose

Grace Is Where I Live: Writing as a Christian Vocation

In Season and Out

Standing Ground: A Personal Story of Faith and Environmentalism

120 Significant Things Men Should Know . . . but Never Ask About

out walking

*Reflections on Our Place
in the Natural World*

John Leax

A Raven's Ridge Book

Baker Books
A Division of Baker Book House Co
Grand Rapids, Michigan 49516

Published by Raven's Ridge Books
an imprint of Baker Books
a division of Baker Book House Company
P.O. Box 6287, Grand Rapids, MI 49516-6287

Printed in the United States of America

Library of Congress Cataloging-in-Publication Data

Leax, John.
    Out walking : reflections on our place in the natural world / John Leax.
        p.   cm.
    ISBN 0-8010-1197-3
    1. Nature—Religious aspects—Christianity. I. Title.
BR115.N3L43   2000
814'.54—dc21   99-058138

For current information about all releases from Baker Book House, visit our web site:
http://www.bakerbooks.com

For Linda

On this the evening of the first of May
in my fifty-sixth year,
I am comforted to know:

that just over the ridge above this house,
the Wiscoy breaks around a small island,
cutting a hole deep beneath the roots
of a cottonwood older than I am:

that in the cool darkness
flowing there, a brown trout lurks,
waiting for night to fall:

that in the woodlot under a dying ash,
the bloodroot that woke
to morning and drank light all day
have curled into themselves:

that in a gray tree, safe
in the middle of a hidden beaver pond,
a heron lays its long beak
on the side of the tangled sticks
of its nest and sleeps:

that in the back yard,
the peepers ring the pond
with single-minded song
and cry the streets
with news the nations need to hear:

that your touch wakes a wildness in my body
older than the words we use
to make our joy complete:

that you, in waking what is lost in me,
preserve the world
until the promised resurrection comes
and all is gathered into love.

contents

prologue

MY BOOTS CRUNCHED on the crust of snow but did not break through, and I pulled my hood up against the wet half snow that fell as I started my February walk through the woodlot. I had been too long away. Subzero temperatures had kept me home and mostly indoors for nearly two months. At last I was out to see how my trees were faring, to see if the heavy snow and ice had broken them as they had broken the lawn trees in town, to see if widow makers waited in the treetops to end my labor on the ground. None did; my trees had fared well, and I walked easily, enjoying the radiance of the wet light under the leafless canopy. As I walked I grew more and more content, more and more at home, settled and pleased to be the caretaker of this wood.

I grew up at the edge of a wood in the midst of a large extended family. My grandparents, four aunts and uncles, and I don't know how many cousins and second cousins all lived along a dirt lane that bore our family name. The lane ran beside a small stream, turned up a steep hill through woods, and then cut sideways just below a cleared ridge that was usually planted in corn. Our house was on the low side of the road. A deep ravine sliced the edge from our back yard. A short path switched back and forth down its side into the second-growth hardwood that isolated us on our hill.

For the first seven years of my life those woods were my playground. My cousins and second cousins were my playmates. We were a scruffy bunch, born just before and just after the Second World War. I don't remember toys other than cap guns or dolls. But toys didn't matter, for we ranged like the untamed animals we were in the woods. It was a good life full of lessons both moral and practical.

My task walking in the woodlot snow reminded me of a small incident. I must have been about six, for I was definitely a follower bending to the influence of my cousins and an uncle just a few years older than I. They roamed farther afield than I and knew deep places in the stream where one could swim. They carried hatchets and small axes in leather sheaths bought at the Boy Scout department in the small department store two towns away. These weapons were a crucial part of their equipment, necessary for *hacking*, one of their favorite pastimes. Hacking involved running through the woods whacking great chunks of bark from the maples and oaks, leaving a trail of white, bleeding blazes to mark a wanton passage. I begged my uncle to take me along. I wanted to hack my way through the woods the way he did.

But he looked at the rubber hatchet I brandished and laughed. "Get a real hatchet," he said, "and you can come."

When my father came home from work that afternoon, I asked for his hatchet, the one he used to chop the heads from the chickens I helped him slaughter. "What for?" he asked.

"I want to go hacking," I answered.

He returned me a puzzled look. "What is hacking?"

"Chopping trees," I replied.

"Are you building something?" he asked.

I began to sense something was wrong. "No," I answered, looking at my feet. "Hacking is just chopping trees."

"Whatever gave you that idea?" he asked.

"Uncle Butch," I answered. "He said I could go with him. Can I have the hatchet?"

"You don't chop trees without a reason," he said and turned away.

I look off through the pattern of tree trunks rising before me. I am amazed that such a small incident has stayed with me, that it comes back so vividly after fifty years. But more than that, I am amazed at my father's wisdom. He taught so lightly I did not know he was teaching. That day he shaped my conscience. Like Christ speaking a parable, he did not even explain. He spoke instead out of his character and placed in my mind an unshakable sense of the meaning of stewardship: the earth is not mine to use as I please.

I understand his words now, and as I walk, I echo them with words older than his, "The earth is the Lord's and the fullness thereof."

out walking

two cheers for technology

EVERY VISIT I'VE MADE to Niagara Falls has been shaped by a book I read in second grade. In *Paddle-to-the-Sea* Holling Clancy Holling narrates the journey of an Indian boy's toy canoe from a snowbank north of Lake Superior through the Great Lakes, down the Saint Lawrence River, across the Atlantic to France, and back to its starting point. Except for a full-color drawing of Niagara Falls bisected by a rainbow, I loved the book. A close look at that drawing reveals a minuscule canoe, a mere dot of red, just beginning its drop from the lip of the fall. The smallness of the canoe against the watery vastness terrified me and plunged me into years of nightmares.

The first time I stood at the edge of the Horseshoe Falls, I saw that toy canoe and I felt dizzy. The same thing happened on a recent Saturday, when I took the students in my class "Writing about Nature and the Environment" to the falls to observe the interactions of nature and culture so evident in the park.

Soaked by the spray, I stood beside an equally wet student in an angle of the railing so close to the falls I felt we could reach our hands into the water. She looked at me and shouted innocently over the roar, "I'd like to throw a leaf in and watch it go over." My stomach twisted.

We turned away, rounded up her classmates, and joined the line for the Journey behind the Falls. An hour later we donned yellow, garbage-bag raincoats and started down the six-hundred-foot tunnel under the falls. I felt a strange confusion, a synesthesia, for I could not be sure if I heard or felt the roar of the falls. At the end of the tunnel, I stood beside the same young woman I'd stood with above. Together we stared into the rush of water. I tried to make out something through it, but I could not. Neither could I discern any pattern to the movement. I turned to my student and said, "It's like staring into Nothing."

A family group came up behind us. I was about to move aside when the mother exclaimed, "It's just like the last place." Husband and children pivoted and marched off.

How much longer my student and I stood there I don't know. Even if I wore a watch, I doubt if it could have measured the niche of eternity we occupied. When others arrived, we retreated through the tunnel and stepped into the deluge of spray on the observation deck at the foot of the falls.

I stood alone as near to the falls as I could get, leaned on the railing, and repeated to myself, "It's like staring into Nothing." And then I remembered Thomas Merton explaining in one of his essays that when Eastern mystics speak of emptiness or nothing, they mean something very much like what a Western mystic means by fullness. I spoke again to myself, "It's like staring into the Fullness."

The wind whipped around me, and I realized I was, once again, drenched. Laughter rose up in me, and I looked for my students. They too were soaked and elated. It was getting late, and our lunches were in the car. We rode the elevator back to the rim of the gorge and ate at a picnic table beside the rose garden.

The next morning, the interaction of nature and culture hit me. My moment of enlightenment, my perception of the fullness of creation, was much like my previous terror at the plunge of Paddle-to-the-Sea. That one of these experiences resulted from reading a book and the other from walking through a marvel of engineering made no difference. Both were responses to cultural artifacts.

I felt betrayed. And then I caught myself. So what if each experience was contrived? Each was also real. Culture, through the technology of the book and the technology of the tunnel, had prepared a way for me to know concretely a truth I might otherwise have never learned.

16

a God to thank

THE SUMMER OF 1998, what was to be the summer of butterflies, became, almost without my noticing, the summer of thankfulness. Our garden, planted with buddleia, nicotiana, coneflowers, bee balm, and other attractors, was well established. We had feeders, water, basking rocks, and we had binoculars handy, holding the field guide closed in the wind. The butterflies came as we hoped: painted ladies, red and white admirals, tiger swallowtails, cabbage whites, sulphurs, blues, and monarchs.

Though I remembered catching, killing, and mounting butterflies in my boyhood, the individuals nectaring on my flowers were safe. My only desire was to know more about them. For me that inevitably leads to books. Through July, my wife and I sat on the deck reading life histories and watching. To broaden my reading, I bought a poem sequence, *The Monarchs* by Alison Hawthorne Deming, the great-great-granddaughter of Nathaniel. I wasn't sure what I was getting when I bought it. I didn't know if it would be God-haunted or simple description. It was neither. It was a complex sequence using the life history of the monarch to examine human experience.

About halfway through it I read these lines.

> Unable to hear, see, smell, or taste,
> they know when to drop their lower branches,
> broaden their root anchor, when to
> climb and bud. The redwoods, without
> liquid hydrogen or God, have mastered time.

I put the book down and stared off at the distant hills. The casual dismissal of God disturbed me. It felt out of place, unnecessary to the poem. Recalling similar passages in Deming's essays, I wondered what Grandfather Nat would think. Then I asked myself what I thought.

Such dismissals occur quite often in the work of recent American nature writers. Biologists seem to lag behind the physicists in the discovery of humility. Their thinking smacks of an arbitrariness akin to Bertrand Russell's. In *Why I Am Not a Christian* Russell complained that if something had to be without a cause, it might as well be the universe as God. At eighteen that appealed to me. Like the physicists, however, I've discovered that my imagination is a little too small to contain the creation. The appearance of chance—even the operation of chance in the universe—does not rule out a pattern I have not yet discovered, or more likely a pattern I cannot discover, for I am a part of it.

About the same time I was reading Russell, I was also reading F. Scott Fitzgerald. No paragon of faith, Fitzgerald articulated a much richer idea. He wrote that though he had never desired a God to pray to, he had often desired a God to thank. I missed much of Fitzgerald's wry humor back there in the early sixties, but his remark has stayed with me, and I've come to cherish it. For now I see that if I admit my life is a gift, I also admit that it is received from a gift-giver to whom I owe a debt of gratitude.

A flutter of orange rose above the hedge, dipped down to the nicotiana, lifted quickly, and then settled on the bee balm: a monarch. I picked up the binoculars and brought him close to my eyes. He was good to see.

Several months have passed since that July day. As Thanksgiving approaches I find myself wondering how to pay that debt of gratitude I feel for my life. I think I begin with my garden, tending it not only for my pleasure but for the well being of the earth itself. Part of that tending is to hold in my imagination, as I held in my binoculars a single butterfly, a mass of monarchs clustered on a particular tree somewhere near the Mexican border. I begin also with my marriage. In a time of scandal and shame, I celebrate in private and public the covenant I have made with one woman and with all women. And I begin in the mystery of the desire for a God to thank. In the humility of that small motion toward faith, I enter the invisible order that harmonizes all I cannot know.

dead squirrels
and mushroom dreams

THROUGH MY YOUTH, after we moved from Leax Lane, I lived in a
house on the edge of a field that abruptly plummeted into a strip mine.
From our back lawn we could see, miles away, the glow of coke ovens.
Around us, extraction was a way of life. Though my grandfather was a dairy
farmer, he was also the owner of a coal mine. It opened conveniently from
a door in his basement, making stoking the furnace easy and the raising of
mushrooms an obligation. I was not allowed to venture far from the light
of the doorway, but I loved the mine's damp dark, and to this day I feel and
smell it when I eat mushrooms.

Growing up, I read *Outdoor Life*, *Field and Stream*, and *Sports Afield*. My
favorite author was the sportsman, columnist, and novelist Robert Ruark.
I dreamed of following his footsteps to writing big books and shooting big
game. To my mind, nature existed for profit, and animals existed as tests
to prove one's nerve, to decorate one's den, and to be worn as coats, belts,
and boots.

Underneath the surface of that violent world, however, a quieter way
waited for me to waken to its promise. I remember my father standing
silently, shaking his head at the mine-ruined creeks where no fish swam.
And I remember Ruark writing not only of trophies but of the foolishness
of shooting down a covey of quail. I can't describe my awakening to this
quieter way, for that awakening occurred at a level beneath my con-
sciousness, but two incidents that surely played a part in it stay with me.

19

A shooting accident in the family that led my father to give up hunting kept me out of the woods until the advent of bow hunting in the mid-fifties. Shooting a forty-five-pound hickory recurve, I became a fairly good instinctive shooter, but my silent safaris proved fruitless. My bow packed a wallop, but its cast was slow. Squirrels simply dodged. Then one day I learned to shoot the instant a squirrel launched itself from a limber branch. The slight slowing of the leap by the branch's give was all the edge I needed. I began to hit squirrels in the air. But no one would cook my triumphs; with nothing to do with the carcasses, I left them in the woods. One day I cut the tail from one and pinned it to my hat. Then a friend's sister scolded me for wearing the dead, gray flag. Shamed, I removed it and gave up shooting squirrels.

The second incident I connect with my awakening came within months of the first. I was panfishing with my father and one of his friends. The friend, on catching a bluegill, would rip the hook free and toss the fish under the boat seat, where it would flop wildly before slowly expiring, the bright colors of its slab side turning dull as it died.

I was appalled.

I liked eating fish. (I still do.) But having learned shame when I killed wantonly, I had learned to hate cruelty. I said nothing, but my expression gave away my thoughts, for the friend laughed and revealed himself a disciple of Descartes. "They don't feel anything," he said and tossed another bluegill to the floor.

What the two incidents have in common is each was a kind of extraction, a profligate mining of the creation for momentary gratification. Both the particular pleasure I received from shooting squirrels and the cruelty of my father's friend denied the possibility of any binding relationship with the creatures other than that of tyrant and slave.

The basement of my house doesn't open into a mine, but it's unheated, dirt, and dark. Mushrooms might do well there.

a just expression of hope

WHEN I BOUGHT my five-acre woodlot and named it Remnant Acres, my intention was to serve it by yielding control of it to a wisdom other than my own. From the beginning, however, my intention has been weak. Circumstances—I need wood for my woodstove—and temperament—I covet a private place to write—have prevented my letting go.

The first year I owned the land, I harvested hemlock, poplar, and a small amount of ash cut and left by the previous owner. The clearing he had made grew up into an impenetrable berry tangle that I stayed out of. Frequently that first summer deer bolted from its cover, reminding me I was the intruder when I passed through. The clearing was an edge, a habitat, and Remnant Acres deserved its name. But the hemlock, poplar, and ash ran out in early March. In spring I walked the woods with firewood on my mind, and then my writer's dream kicked in. On Memorial Day I bought an old camper and towed it to the edge of the clearing between the hemlocks and the berry tangle. Through the summer I sat in the airiness of its screen and canvas walls and wrote. Occasionally that summer, walking the narrow path to the camper, I spooked a deer. In the fall I folded the camper back into itself and left the woods.

This alternation of presence and absence continued for several years. Then, desiring to work through winter, I tore out the canvas and sided the camper. I became, without warrant, a resident of the woodlot. When I go there now, I see deer trails, worn and marked with fresh tracks, but deer no longer stop; they pass through. This change is small, but it is important. It suggests that human possession of a place tends to be exclusive.

The flood story of Genesis ends with a chilling statement. God says to Noah, whose virtue has led to the salvation of creation, that all creatures will go in fear of him. Though this statement has long troubled me, I am beginning to understand. God's statement is not an order creating division; it is a recognition of the human fallenness that brought him to flood the earth. Fear is a gift to the creatures, a protection from humanity's rapacity.

For most of history this fear, and the fear that humans felt in return, was all the protection the creatures needed. This mutual and sustaining fear, however, is no longer sufficient. The fate of all creatures now depends on humanity's willingness to restrain itself, to commit itself to maintain places where humans pass through. Though I had this intention in mind when I named Remnant Acres, I failed to acknowledge the inevitability of changing circumstances. I made an inadequate commitment.

Consider an analogy. As part of the marriage ceremony, a couple promises, before God and gathered witnesses, to be faithful to each other until separated by death. This promise is not demanded by sentiment; it is demanded because everyone present at the marriage knows the truth of human nature. Both bride and groom will change. Ambitions, new dreams, other bodies will attract them. Their only hope for success will be the reach of their vow.

This is the lesson of Remnant Acres and the deer's passage. We must marry the earth. We must promise to cherish and serve it (love it as ourselves) until death releases us from our responsibility. Our lives will change. We will be tempted. Apart from such a marriage, a commitment to limit our use of the earth before we know or imagine all possible uses, the earth and all of us on it are lost, for that commitment is our only just expression of hope.

on the average

ON A THURSDAY AFTERNOON in mid-November, I hauled my last cord of wood home from the woodlot. Though brittle leaves curled from beneath the dust of snow and more snow was predicted to fall that evening, I did not hurry. I gave myself up to the day.

A couple of weeks before, I'd cut a misshapen ash I'd been threatening for a long time. It had grown a kind of shoulder about two feet from the ground and had stretched three trunks from it. The largest was about twelve inches in diameter. The bark where the trunks rubbed each other had peeled loose several years ago and had fallen away. Last spring only a few branches budded, and over the summer, deadwood showed clearly in the canopy.

From a hundred yards away, I saw the white end of a log shining like a grounded moon from the dark leaves pooled around the stump. From it, broken lines of stove wood, like moonshine on rippled water, trailed across the woods floor. I pushed my cart to the far end of the illusion and started loading. It took seven trips to load the truck, and as I warmed to the work, I would have enjoyed a colder day.

Friday morning, when I went to my desk to prepare for my afternoon class on the interactions of nature and culture, I experienced one of those moments of congruence that always come as a surprise to those whose work is sharply divided between the labor of the mind and the labor of the body. I opened my text to Aldo Leopold's essay "Axe-in-Hand" and began to read. "When some remote ancestor of ours invented the shovel, he became a giver: he could plant a tree. And when the axe was invented, he became a taker: he could chop it down."

Slowly I read on. All thoughts of class preparation slipped from my mind as I read Leopold's eloquent examination of the bias that leads him to favor one tree over another in his woodlot. I thought of my own bias, and I remembered walking through the woods several springs ago with my wife, Linda. I'd pointed out the three-trunked ash.

"That one will have to go," I said.

"No," she answered. "It's interesting. Cut the straight ones; they're only good for money."

Leopold would have enjoyed our discussion. "It is a matter of what a man thinks about while chopping, or deciding what to chop," he wrote, anticipating the quiet clash of my wife's bias and mine.

As I remembered that conversation, I returned, in my imagination, to the woods. Where the grounded moon lay beside the stump, I saw a white patch of bloodroot. Regret rose up in me. When I'd cut the ash, thinking only of firewood, I'd forgotten how every May, when the air feels just right, I know, without thinking, that spring has taken hold, and I walk into the woods and stand beneath that three-trunked tree and rejoice in the flood of bloodroot spreading in the filtered light of the budding canopy.

Now, as I wait out the winter, I wonder what I have done. Will the bloodroot bloom this spring? What if it depends on that slant of light falling through the ash for its recurrence? Will it be gone? Thinking these thoughts, I returned to Leopold and found in his conclusion a kind of comfort. "Such are the pros and cons the wielder of an axe must foresee, compare, and decide upon with calm assurance that his bias will, on the average, prove to be something more than good intentions."

Slowly light lengthens and takes hold. Soon, I will know.

spit in the wind

BEFORE DRIVING to Cape Cod for a meeting of writers the last weekend of February, I'd read several books on the area: Thoreau's *Cape Cod*, Henry Beston's *The Outermost House*, John Hay's *The Great Beach*, and Robert Finch's *Common Ground*. My friends at the meeting said I'd overprepared. They may have been right, for as I walked the beaches, I wasn't sure if I was experiencing the Cape or the words of writers.

This confusion impressed itself on me the first afternoon as my wife and I sauntered along the beach at Rock Harbor. The tide was low, the sun was out, and the bay was calm. Where we walked, the beach was littered with the empty shells of razor clams, mussels, and crabs. Occasionally we'd find half a gull or a cluster of feathers. My wife, a normally cheerful person, surprised me when she said, "Everything here is dead."

"Yes," I answered, "Thoreau called the shore a great morgue."

Later that afternoon, Robert Finch read to us. He began with some casual remarks about the dolphin stranding at Wellfleet earlier in the month. Because I'd seen television coverage of the event, I was prepared for a salvation narrative. Instead he told us of holding a dolphin in his arms while a veterinarian euthanized it. Then he read a troubling meditation on strandings and the human need to understand the seemingly pointless horrors of the natural world.

Cape Cod, made of glacial moraine and sand, moves and changes. As Finch read, my thoughts blew and shifted. No matter how I wished it otherwise, my sight was focused by the words of writers.

My confusion continued the next day when I hiked Coast Guard Beach. I chose that hike for several reasons. It was moderately long. At the end of it, I had a reasonable chance of finding harbor seals. And it was the location where in 1925 Henry Beston had perched the Outermost House on a dune overlooking the Atlantic.

Beston's book was with me as I walked: I had it in my pocket. It did not, however, help me see Nauset Spit. The exposed finger of sand rising between the Atlantic and the Nauset Marsh would not yield its reality to old words. It was too changed. The winter hurricane of 1978 had swept the house and the dune away. The soft sand that remained pulled at my feet. Before I'd gone two hundred yards, I was tired. But the day was warm with almost no wind. Finding a rhythm and a line of firmer footing, I settled into enjoying myself.

I don't know how far I walked. One of my sources reports the spit is a mile long. Another grants it two miles. About halfway down it, I found a group of walkers gathered around a single harbor seal. It lay on its back so motionless it could have been dead. It wasn't. One of the walkers, longing for some cross-species communication, reached out to scratch its belly. Like a single muscle it recoiled, turned on him, and snarled, baring dangerous teeth. I left the group to its nervous laughter and followed the beach to the end of the spit.

The wind came up as I returned. The Coast Guard station looked very far away, and I thought of Beston making this walk in the fog, in the rain, and in the blowing snow of a northeaster. Suddenly I felt very exposed. The Outermost House was no Walden. Here on a spit in the wind, Beston had met what Thoreau described as "a force not bound to be kind to man."

The next day, the wind came up. I got in my car and drove through rain to Albany. I did not go back to see the surf as the storm rolled in. It was enough to know that ahead of me, between my night's rest and home, it was dumping twenty inches of snow on Syracuse. As I drove, my legs were tight and sore from the walk, reminding me of the harsh reality of the shifting sands and the looseness of our hold on this wonderful, terrifying world.

telescopes, comets,
and stones

WHEN I WAS A BOY, I spent a lot of evenings trying to match the patterns on a star map with those in the sky. I was never successful. The gift of a telescope only narrowed my vision to points of light that told me nothing. In college, given a choice, I studied geology. I figured if I couldn't know the far away, I'd give the up close a look.

Recently I read an account of Thoreau's first glimpse at the sky through a telescope. He was pleased to learn that as of 1850 astronomers still valued the naked eye. Though my imagination has been pretty well reconfigured by the photographs taken from the Hubble telescope, like Thoreau, I want to think my eye is still some good. Perhaps that is why I missed my chance to see Halley's comet when it passed by several years ago.

Alfred University had opened its observatory to anyone who wanted to see the comet during the fall. Knowing that in the spring it would be visible to the unaided eye, I chose to stay home. When I made that choice, I did not know the spring window for viewing the fleeting iceball would last only one week, that the hours for viewing it would be from 3 to 5 a.m., and that it would be visible only if the sky were absolutely cloudless.

This is western New York.

It snowed. All week.

And so tonight, several years later, under a clear sky, I sit writing about what might have been.

Snyder Hill rises from the Genesee valley to the east of Fillmore. An electric cross, lit every Christmas and Easter, stands at its top. During the early 1970s, every Sunday morning, my wife, my young daughter, and I traveled over it to the Short Tract United Methodist Church. On the way home, cresting the hill at the foot of the cross was like being born into a new world. Miles of valley burst into our sight as the car, which had been pointing skyward, suddenly tilted forward and plunged toward the river. Some mornings the light was so dazzling we pulled off the road and sat without talking.

Though Snyder Hill has on occasion been the site of a community Easter sunrise service, I've never been to one. Easter is usually too cold a morning to rouse me hours early from my quiet sleep. I understand the resurrection celebrates the triumph of the body's heat over the coldness of the grave, but the grim freezing that would take place on Snyder Hill, in spite of the joyous proclamation of the morning, is for me too strong a reminder that though one grave has been opened, mine is still to be dug. That, however, is another story.

My plan, all those years ago, was to view Halley's comet from the foot of the cross on Snyder Hill the morning of the spring equinox. It would have been a wonderful conjunction. That neither I nor the comet showed and the snow did reminds me that the Lord called those who asked for a sign "a wicked and perverse generation," and I am a little chagrined.

As I think on it, my missing the comet is not without its own value as a sign. When I wrote "neither I nor the comet showed," I was being flip. My lack of vision, my being lost in a cloud of snow, had nothing to do with the comet; it was there flaming across the sky. I did not see it because, when I was graciously offered sight, I preferred to see with my own eyes. I should have known: from the foot of the cross, the sky is always dark.

Fortunately, I still have geology. A curious stone demands consideration.

close encounters

LINDA AND I WORKED on the garden in the morning, taking chances, planting early. In the afternoon we loaded the canoe on the truck and headed to Silver Lake. The wind was up, but that didn't matter, for as soon as we put in, we paddled to the south end of the lake, slid the canoe over the muddy bar, and entered the marsh.

Out of the wind, the water was smooth. We made no sounds as I paddled and Linda glassed the shores. Red-winged blackbirds raised a ruckus and teetered on bobbing cattails. Grackles foraged and fished at the water's edge. Beautiful birds, native, iridescent and handsome, they are maligned and judged guilty by their association with the upstart starlings. Cedar waxwings flocked in a row of trees. A few mallards, both hens and drakes, puttered along behind us, circling in a watery holding pattern when we stopped to watch a yellow warbler.

Besides these there was a large kingfisher-sized bird we could not identify no matter how we searched through our Peterson guidebook. As we sat drifting, teased by the nearness of the unknown bird, I read Peterson's comforting words to Linda, "Do not be embarrassed if you cannot name *every* bird you see. . . . It is the mark of an expert to occasionally put a question mark after certain birds on his list."

"Occasionally," said Linda and laughed.

A sudden eruption in the water ahead startled us, and we rocked the canoe turning to see. Large ripples washed across the channel. What had made them was gone. When the water next erupted, we were facing the right direction. Fifty yards away something large rolled and thrashed. Loops of flesh rose and fell in and out of the water. What we saw appeared to be six or eight inches thick and eight to ten feet long. It twisted and turned like something out of a National Geographic special.

I started paddling toward it.

"What are you doing?" Linda protested.

"Going to see," I answered.

Although we both knew we hadn't seen what we had seen, thoughts of alligator-wrestling anacondas and the Loch Ness Monster rolled through our heads. As we neared the place of the disturbance, the Silver Lake Sea Serpent seemed a possibility, and, I admit, we were both foolishly apprehensive. At the center of the ripples, we found only muddy water.

A few moments later, however, the water was again broken by the twisting creature. This time we were a bit closer, and we saw not one monster but several. They were six to eight inches thick, but they weren't eight feet long. They were northern pike, two to three feet long, trying to occupy the same territory in the warm shallow water.

We found them all along the winding channel. One butted the canoe bottom as we passed. I brushed another with the paddle in a narrow spot. They were big fish. As I watched them, I remembered in my hands their thrilling liveliness at the end of a line. But I had no desire to tackle one. Their fearful presence in the water moved me closer to awe than any triumph I've collected with rod and reel.

Reluctantly, we returned to the lake. Far down the shoreline a great blue heron stood motionless in the water. His neck curved back, poised to strike. We watched for several minutes before he lifted one foot above the surface, reached it forward, and slipped it without a ripple back into the water. He moved four steps and stopped. When he struck, he struck so swiftly we missed it. He swallowed quickly, stretching his neck straight and shaking his head. Then he resumed his dangerous stillness.

Newly awake, the wind in our faces, we slapped through the small waves. All the way back our hearts thrummed alert as the heron's, as wild as the northern's.

30

a particular dove

THE FLEDGLING MOURNING DOVE huddled, disturbing the dust of my neighbor's driveway as well as my neighbor. Having been called by my wife, I stood sipping my morning coffee. I'd seen the dove the day before. It had hopped ahead of me, dragging its right wing, as I spaded the garden along the hedge. Watching it then, I'd thought about the five neighborhood cats and its slight chance of survival. I was surprised to find it still alive.

A hint of panic colored my neighbor's voice when she spoke. "It can't fly. What should we do?"

"There's not much we can do," I answered, but the expressions I looked at told me I needed to do something. "A wildlife rehabilitator might take it," I said. "But I don't know one. I guess we could catch it and try to tend it ourselves."

"I called a pet store," my neighbor said. "They told me it's illegal to keep wild birds."

I knew that, but legality wasn't my concern. One way or the other, the dove was going to die. We could cage it and watch it starve, or we could abandon it to the cats. I didn't want to do either. To kill time, I went and got a box, picked up the bird, and carried it to temporary safety. Then I went back to my coffee. Sitting in my office later that morning, I stared out the window and watched whales in the clouds.

Several years ago, I watched, along with the rest of the world, the drama of three whales trapped by ice in the Beaufort Sea. Nightly, network television broadcast footage of efforts to free them. Men with chainsaws cut futilely at the ice. Witnesses talked emotionally of how it felt to be helpless spectators. And all of us, viewers, news reporters, and wildlife advocates, cheered when a Russian icebreaker cleared a channel and the whales swam free.

Had the news cameras not stumbled across those whales, they might have been discovered, killed, and incorporated into the native economy. A polar bear might have happened upon them and feasted. Or they might have quietly drowned. In each case they would have nourished another life, one nature cares for as impersonally as it cares for the whales. Our imagination and empathy interrupted that cycle.

Sometime during those days glued to the television, I asked myself some questions. Why were we so concerned about these particular whales? Why, after nearly eradicating whales for profit, were we spending so much money to rescue three? What, exactly, did all the hoopla mean?

I didn't answer the questions then, but staring out the window with the dove on my mind, I began to suspect the three questions share one answer: the human imagination is particular. One whale, facing imminent death, has more power to move us than a species facing extinction.

I am tempted to say that we are sentimentalists. We may be, but I do not think that sentimentality is the issue. The issue is learning to extend our care from an individual to a species. The empathy we feel in the face of particular suffering seems to be a logical starting point. But taken by itself it is not enough, for it does not comprehend the harsh reality of nature's apparent indifference. Nature, like it or not, is not particular. It struck me, as I watched the whales in the sky shift shapes and turn into camels and weasels, that perhaps I needed to learn, not nature's indifference, but something of her larger concern, something of how particular deaths (even mine) fit into a pattern of exchange and nourish the health of creation.

Thinking that thought, I pushed my chair back, got up, and drove home. Without telling anyone, I took the dove to a sumac-covered bank behind the house, released it, turned my back, and walked away.

understanding mrs. keister

THE SUMMER I WAS TWELVE, my parents bought four treeless acres—
a fragment of a hillside pasture—from Mrs. Keister, a widowed farm wife,
and built their dream house. Though they immediately set about planting,
my brother and I had to range off of our property to find a tree to climb. In
the interval between our hill and the rise behind us, about a quarter mile
from the windows of Mrs. Keister, we found two mature black walnuts. The
lowest branches of each were far above our heads. We promptly nailed
boards up the trunk of the larger one to make a ladder.

In the fall we blackened our hands gathering the nuts, and the next
spring we started a tree house. Using old clothesline, we hauled a sheet of
plywood fifteen feet up into the tree and more or less leveled it across two
branches. Then we built walls and a roof. When we were done, the shack
had a rakish, devil-may-care look that we were proud of.

Then the phone call came.

Mrs. Keister was not happy.

Neither was my father. "Boys," he said, "Mrs. Keister wants your tree
house down."

We protested, "Why?"

He answered, "There are things in life we never understand."

The next day, as if offering sympathy, he helped us remove it—right
down to the ladder on the trunk.

A few weeks ago, several of the neighborhood boys discovered an appealing storage shed and decided to make it into a clubhouse.

We watched, amused and distressed, as the contents accumulated on the grass. We breathed relief when they were hauled away, and we laughed when Christmas lights appeared twinkling on the July eves.

Distress returned when we came home one day to find the roof stripped and clouds gathering. Then, about eleven that night, I looked out my bedroom window and saw a huge figure bearing a roll of tar paper, backlit by a trouble light, rise slowly over the roof of the shed. As thunder rolled in the distance, the figure quickly laid down a tenuous covering, and I shook my head in amazement.

The next day, the boys shingled the roof. Currently they're painting, and I hear from one of them they've planted grass.

Mrs. Keister, I am sure, would not be happy. I'm a bit bothered because I'm beginning to understand her. Convention and respectability count for a lot in this strange, pride-filled world we adults maintain.

Recent writers on childhood and nature have explored the importance of forts, clubhouses, and shacks to the development of character and self. Evidence suggests that children learn more than how to pound nails when they engage in these projects. Free from adult supervision, investing their energy in making a place of their own, children learn independence and the limits of independence. They learn to relate to each other. Just as important, they learn their relationship to the place they simultaneously make and discover. Without comprehending these relationships, children cannot grow into neighbors who care both for each other and for the place where they live.

Before we built our tree house, my brother and I had another shack, a neat one my father had built for us. It stood beside a small creek in a second growth woods near our first home. What I remember most about it now is how small it was. Though my father had designed it, he had to stoop to enter it. I believe that was his plan, for I think he understood an adult entering the world of a child needs to put off the habit of standing tall to measure up in the neighborhood watch. I think he also understood that is the way one enters the kingdom of heaven. Thinking of that kingdom, I am struck by a devilish thought: should some of those mansions in heaven be tree houses, I pray one with a rakish roofline was saved for Mrs. Keister.

heron watch

EARLY IN JULY three summers ago, I learned the location of a heron rookery. It was small: two nests—wild tangles of large sticks that looked quite uncomfortable—in a single, dead tree standing in the middle of a beaver pond. Two young occupied each nest. They were quite large, fully fledged, past feeding from their parents' bills, and looked to be nearly ready to be on their own. The four birds were likely survivors of a grim competition; two or three others had probably been forced from each nest by those I saw.

The following spring, I began making regular trips to the rookery. Snow remained in the shadows of the woods when I found each nest occupied by a heron. They were still, their necks folded back, their long beaks too bright, almost orange rather than the yellow shown in my field guide.

I watched a long time before one finally rose and stood on the side of the nest. She shrugged, seeming to double her body size as her wings fluffed out. She ran her beak up and down opposite sides of the tree trunk as if she were honing a knife blade on a sharpening rod. Then she flew. I assumed I was looking at females, but I couldn't really know. Herons can be sexed from a distance only by their position while mating.

By mid-April six birds were frequenting the pond and the tree. I watched one day as two pairs worked to line the nests. One bird tore white-pine needles from a tree near me, flew back to the nest, and passed them to its mate. The mate tucked the material into the lining, seemed to register some

35

sort of satisfaction, and then flew off to a pine on the other side of the pond. It returned with more needles and passed them to the first bird, who in turn tucked them into the sticks. The second pair followed the same procedure, but they seemed to be using grass for the lining.

After that, though I went regularly to the pond, nothing much seemed to be going on. Either I'd find the nests empty, or I'd find the birds nestled down in them so only the yellow lines of their beaks resting on the sides were visible. My watching, frankly, grew tedious. Whatever those birds were doing, they were doing it on their own time. That didn't bother me too much. Sitting there, however, day after day, my eyes stuck to the binoculars, watching from four hundred yards away, I began to feel slightly perverse, as if I were some kind of Peeping Tom spying on my neighbors. Something I did not understand was wrong.

In mid-June I went away, and I did not return until the nests were empty. This year I did not go back at all.

Recently, reading theologian Sallie McFague, I discovered what was bothering me. In *Super, Natural Christians* she writes, "Staring at others as if they were in a fishbowl or a zoo: this is what Sigmund Freud called scopophilia—subjecting other people to a curious, controlling gaze, seeing them as objects." Scopophilia at its most perverse, of course, is pornography. My gazing was relatively innocent, and I do not question the necessary observation of science, but my gazing was curious and self-oriented. I wanted to know about herons so I could (as I am doing now) write about my experience with herons. I did not want to know them as themselves. I know this because I wrote in my notes, "I realize that what I am doing is only partially about a desire to explore and enter the life of another creature. I realize that that desire in and of itself may be merely another form of tourism or exploitation."

I have not stopped watching herons, but I no longer seek them out. I watch instead for moments when our lives come together, for moments when we can be neighborly, when we can greet each other without the prying curiosity of the gossip who would peel off the layers of appropriate privacy for the sake of a story.

36

boomerang salamanders
and hummingbird bugs

FOR FOUR DAYS in August I played host to my six-year-old nephew, Ryan. When he arrived, I was working through an unpleasantly heavy book of literary criticism. Its author argues that American nature writers are unique, for they seek to organize information and observations into a knowable world by combining the traditional form of spiritual autobiography with scientific language.

Not remembering much about six-year-olds, I tucked the book under my arm and set out with him for the stream on my woodlot. I thought I'd get to sit and read while he turned over rocks and caught salamanders. It didn't happen that way. Ryan set our agenda. "You lift the rocks, I'll grab the salamanders," he said. For two hours I lifted, and he grabbed. He missed a few, and a couple lost tails, but most he caught by the neck, held up to examine, and placed gently in the big, white bucket I carried.

"I think salamanders are cute, don't you Uncle Jack?" he asked. A good professor, I quibbled with his word choice and said, "They're sleek and beautiful." Though Ryan kept picking larger and larger rocks for me to move as the sun warmed the morning, I think I appreciated being in the woods doing nothing useful as much as he did.

Near noon, I persuaded him we had enough captives and suggested he draw them before returning them to the stream. He settled down with his sketch pad and markers on the step of my writing shack, and I leaned back

37

against a tree with my book. Unlike Ryan, however, I didn't settle down. My book aggravated me.

I watched Ryan. He held a salamander and gazed at it with such obvious, awestruck love I could almost imagine the salamander willingly lying down with him like the lion with the lamb. "This one is a boomerang salamander," he said authoritatively.

"That's interesting," I answered.

"See the marks down its back? They're like little boomerangs."

I went back to my book. As I read, I realized the author doesn't think much of nature writers unless they are self-conscious about their work and recognize that it is nothing more than a biological reflex. Most writers, he complains, believe their language is more significant than a cardinal's territorial song. The best nature writers, he insists, know better.

I snapped the book shut just as Ryan exclaimed, "Look! There's a hummingbird bug!"

"What's a hummingbird bug?" I asked.

"It's a bug that flaps its wings so fast you can't see them moving."

"Oh," I said. My reading and the conversation Ryan and I had earlier that morning about the hummingbirds in my garden came together. "Where did you learn that salamander is called a boomerang salamander?" I asked.

"I made it up," he said. Seeing my smile, he tilted his head and knotted his forehead. "It's okay to make up names, isn't it?" he asked.

"Sure," I answered. "You gave it a good name." And he had. His name described the animal and allowed us to hold it in our minds as we talked. As in his naming of the hummingbird bug, he had gathered his knowledge and his observations and imaginatively made his world knowable.

My sociobiologist critic would demur. But he is a reductionist. Believing that human beings are created in the image of God, I am incapable of imagining our language acts as no more significant than a cardinal's call. The sociobiologist, working from purely materialist assumptions, is incapable of imagining that by acts of language human beings connect the objective, physical world with the subjective world of their responses. In naming the salamander, Ryan followed the command given to Adam in the garden. He completed creation by articulating a relationship.

His imaginative naming lacked only one thing—an institutional sanction. We find such sanction in the language of science and the language of faith. Nature writers, joining the two languages, act to bring forth a new way of organizing our knowable world. Creating a new discourse, they create a new community.

The boomerang salamander, by the way, is a mountain dusky salamander. The hummingbird bug I never saw. God knows what it is.

the edible yard

the world of tomorrow

IT'S NEARLY 11 P.M., late for me to be sitting at a typewriter, but I'm away from home, holed up in my room at the George Meany Center for Labor Studies in Silver Spring, Maryland, where I teach writing two weeks a year. I enjoy these weeks. For a short while, I mingle with the working men and women who nurtured me as I grew up, and I get a good dose of the world beyond the book-lined tower of conservative academia. I never go into Washington when I'm here, but I feel close to the action. Bill and Newt are just down the street, not even a pay call away. Once, the proximity overwhelmed me, and I called my congressman; he was out. It didn't matter. The benefits of being so near the nation's heartbeat I most enjoy have nothing to do with politics. I like having my choice of radio stations playing classical music and I enjoy experiencing weather more bizarre than any I have at home.

Right now rain spatters my window, and lightning flashes, striking pink, suggesting something vitally wrong with the air I breathe during my city sojourn, but I can't complain. The air at home isn't so good either. The West Valley Nuclear Reprocessing Center, after all, is only thirty miles due west of my woods along the Genesee, and west of that the power plants of Ohio belch and fume. Along with the lightning, thunder rumbles eloquently, almost obscuring the softer but steady rumble of the beltway a hundred yards out of my sight to the south.

I sit here having outside-the-beltway thoughts. My stomach is uncomfortable from too much rich food, and I've been reading E. B. White's *One Man's Meat* since eight o'clock, when I left a panel discussion on alternate futures. No one attempted any prophecies, but the mood was surprisingly optimistic. Consequently, I kept quiet, keeping my morose broodings on the decline and fall of practically everything to myself.

In "The World of Tomorrow," one of the essays in *One Man's Meat*, White described the mood he encountered at the 1939 World's Fair. The spirit there was even more brightly optimistic than the one I encountered this evening. White's future, however, is now the distant past, and I can venture a few comments on it. In a world where the evening newscast brings me images of Bosnia, Somalia, Lebanon, and Iraq, I read with bitter amusement the narration White quotes from his journey through the Perisphere, "a brave new world . . . built by united hands and hearts. Here brain and brawn, faith and courage, are linked in high endeavor as men march on toward unity and peace. Listen! From office, farm, and factory they come with joyous song."

The only song I've heard this week—I think of the Rachmaninoff piano concerto currently filling the room as something considerably more than a song—was the anthem "Solidarity," sung with linked arms and camp meeting fervor by two hundred labor leaders who, in spite of the democratic administration, know the brave new world has by no means arrived. Apart from that, I've heard mostly snatches of cries for help from the flooded midwest, the parched south, the rusting north, and crumbling California— and the unceasing roar of the traffic on the beltway.

White encountered no cries for help in the world of tomorrow. Neither did he encounter traffic. The futurists of 1939 projected the highways of 1960 (the year I learned to drive) as "ribbons of perfection through the fertile and rejuvenated America." Following the directives in the narration, White imagined "going a hundred miles an hour around impossible turns ever onward."

I drove one of those projected highways on my way to this seat in the window: the Pennsylvania Turnpike. I was a child when it was completed, and I remember enduring a long Sunday drive from Pittsburgh to the Midway Plaza at Breezewood. I endured it because my parents wanted to say they'd driven that nearly miraculous four-lane expanse cut and tunneled through the mountains.

As I drove the highway this week, forty years and more after that ride, most of it was under repair. When I wasn't running at sixty miles per hour watching for troopers, I drove at reduced work-zone speed limits and watched for lane changes and delays. I also drove it watching for a decent place to eat. Finding none, I was forced to choose between eating at McDonald's or going hungry. As I sit here, I wish I'd read White's essay before my trip; I would have watched for signs of the "fertile and rejuvenated America." I saw some mighty nice mountains, but I don't know who owns them, and I don't know if they're rejuvenated. I know the mountains I've seen in Washington state aren't, and I know the recent, much-heralded agreement forged in Washington D.C. to resolve differences between the timber industry and environmentalists isn't going to change that. But who can tell about the future? Maybe I'm just a grouch, and the utopia of the World's Fair is just ahead.

White lived to see 1960. His published letters make it clear he didn't much like the roads or the automobiles on them. I tend to agree. An hour or so ago, I tucked his book under my arm and set off for a nearby chain restaurant and a cup of tea. To reach it, I had to cross New Hampshire Avenue, a six-lane obstacle with all the characteristics of an above-ground supercollider. A construction crew had blocked off the curb lane, so I stepped into the street without watching where I was going and nearly planted my foot on a garter snake. I assume it was a garter snake. It was the right size, but it was dark, and I won't guarantee my hasty identification. What I will guarantee is that I stepped back instinctively. Then I stood watching the snake scrawl its way, a slithering S-shape, toward the eager traffic racing a few feet in front of it.

I thought of bending down, catching the thing up, and placing it in the dry grass behind me, but it was awfully close to the traffic. There was no way, however softhearted I might be, I was going to turn my back on the Hondas, Jaguars, Fords, and Buicks accelerating toward the beltway ramp. I abandoned the snake, went twenty or thirty yards on down the road, and jaywalked.

I had my tea, a miserable, lukewarm brew that not even lemon helped, and retraced my steps. Again, guilty pedestrian that I am, I jaywalked and came up to where I'd last seen the snake. He was still there, a couple of feet farther into the traffic. I stood in the dark and watched a minute or two. Every passing car pounded what was left of its flattened body flatter. Finally, my mind empty of thought, I turned away.

My steps broke the brittle grass, and as I crossed the expanse of lawn to my room, I had a vague feeling I had seen the future.

# of humans and turtles

MY GRANDFATHER MIMNAUGH kept turtles for pets. He drilled holes in their shells near their tails and tethered them to trees with wires. In the evenings, while the adults talked, I watched the turtles at the ends of their wires, straining toward the wild. They seemed to me, somehow, to be older than time, living relics from a prehistory known only to God. My grandfather underscored that idea one evening as he watched my watching. "Turtles," he said, "can live over a hundred years." Then he told a story of finding a turtle down by the river that had the date 1860 carved in its shell. It was 1950. I was seven years old.

A few years later, when my family moved to the country, my brother and I discovered a woods where we sometimes found box turtles burrowed, camouflaged in the leaves. We picked them up—one doesn't catch box turtles; they snap their shells tight and fit the earth like stones when threatened—and carried them home. But we did not drill their shells and wire them to trees. We simply penned them in a plywood frame, kept them for a few days, feeding them strawberries and earthworms, and then returned them to the woods.

The summer I was fifteen or sixteen I dug a small fishpond at the bottom of a terrace in the back yard, planted a water lily, and stocked the water with fancy, fantailed goldfish. Some of those bizarre relatives of the common carp were so overbred to please connoisseurs of the decorative they could hardly swim. One afternoon my brother came home from the aquarium with a sleek painted turtle the size of my hand and turned it loose in my pond.

A turtle on land is a turtle. A turtle in the water is quick. It shot from his hand to the deepest, unreachable part of the pond under the water lily and settled on the bottom, a dark, predatory presence in the watery Eden I had made. Before we caught it, three goldfish died in its jaws. I was angry then; it was my money and my design for nature that turtle was eating. As I sit remembering, however, I am filled with admiration. The natural swiftness of that turtle far outshines my silly fish.

I saw a painted turtle yesterday. It was on the highway north of here, heading from one marsh to another. It ducked its head back into its shell as we straddled it and sped on. The New York Turtle and Tortoise Society encourages drivers to stop and move turtles across the road. Almost half of the 240 species of turtles in the world are threatened. When I mentioned that, my friend, who was driving, offered to go back, but I said no. Another day was too strong in my mind.

Several summers ago, I stopped my car and walked back up a road to rescue a painted turtle. I was about to step into the highway to pick it up when a car approached. I had to wait. For a moment I was anxious. Then I saw that the car was driven by a man I knew, a local businessman and respected member of the community. I relaxed.

Beside me he swerved. I heard the shell pop and felt the spatter of the turtle's life on my bare arms.

I stood in the road and looked at the shattered olive carapace marked with vermillion and yellow. I watched the car vanish around a bend, and I turned from the obscene smear in horror and disgust. I went home and told my wife what had happened. "Are you sure he saw it?" she asked.

Raging, I answered, "He swerved straight at it." But I wanted her to be right. I told no one else, and finally I began to believe it had been an accident. Why, I asked myself, would a man destroy so wantonly? I asked that question rhetorically. But meditating on it over time, I have come to understand it is a real question with no clear answer.

In my grandfather's yard I felt something prehistoric, vaguely threatening, about the turtles. I felt that even more strongly one dusk, bass fishing in a grown-over oxbow of the Genesee River. I had waded waist deep into the water. Bats zoomed about my head, picking off mosquitos, and though the road was only one hundred yards away, I seemed to be in a world apart where anything could happen. That atmosphere affected me and colored the evening as surely as the fallen sun. Something picked up my bait and swam slowly toward the cover of lilies. Pulling like a carp, it did not turn when I set the hook. I thumbed the reel, trusting the drag. It held. The line angled, then went slack. I reeled quickly. Whatever I had caught was swimming to me. About twenty feet away, it surfaced—a plate-sized snapping turtle, a nightcrawler hanging from its jaw. I knew what it could do; I knew its beak could slice to bone. In its domain I felt soft and vulnerable. It came on relentlessly. I stopped reeling, dug my knife from my pocket, and cut it loose. Still coming at me, it dived. Too shocked to move, I watched the dark disk beneath the water. Totally other, as beautiful as the wild itself, it bumped my leg, tilted, and swerved away into blackness. For more than a moment, standing in that water, I was afraid, capable of killing what I feared.

Fear, however, is a passing emotion. Unless it is ingrained and turned to hatred, it is closely related to awe, and awe leads not to destruction but to worship. Deeper than fear, and more destructive, is a prideful refusal to acknowledge any connectedness to the creation. This pride is ultimately gnostic; it denies value to creaturehood and longs for a state of pure spirituality. In its benign form it sings, "This world is not my home." In its malignant form it kills. It is, perhaps, the original sin of the gardeners of Eden.

Frederick Morgan narrates a story similar to what I've told here in his poem "The Turtle." At ten years of age, bird-watching with his mother, he sees two teenagers in a model-T run down a box turtle. He concludes his poem with these lines:

> . . . I've sheltered, since then, a certain hard knowledge
> that has kept me from yielding spirit or mind
> to hopeful assumptions of man's native goodness.

I've always thought Morgan's response too harsh, too much the bitter residue of the loss of innocence. But I've come to think him right. The story of my swerving businessman does not end that day beside the high-way. It continues. This winter everyone was shocked when he emptied his company's bank account, abandoned his family, and skipped town for parts unknown. Somehow, I wasn't surprised. His actions seemed to be of a piece, for I've come to see both the wanton destruction of any creature and the willful manipulation of others as evidence of a nature at odds with nature. It points to that malignancy of spirit that refuses to acknowledge the cre-ated goodness of the body, the inherent beauty of the Creator's flesh and blood. And it points to that malignancy of spirit that refuses responsibil-ity, that chooses to fly off to gratify the isolated self, that has infected humans and threatened turtles since our first failure in the garden.

on mount tamalpais

The dull drone
of the distant city:
the cry of a single bird!

POINT REYES IS BURNING. I've watched the now commonplace
scenes of the fires sweeping through the California chaparral on the evening
news the past two nights. After hiking in the mountains there one afternoon last spring, I better understand what is happening. The fires can't be
stopped. One report I heard argued that, apart from the burned out houses,
the damage to the human community, the fires are actually good for the
area. That may be so, but I doubt it's much comfort to the homeowners
who have invested nearly all their wealth to live in the presence of that
dangerous beauty.

I think of the parable about the man who built his house upon the sand.
When the floods came, it was washed away. In California the sands are real
and metaphorical. Lives are washed away by earthquake, wind, and fire.
But who can resist the stunning beauty of that coast?

A few years ago I visited northern California for the first time. I flew
into San Francisco on a Saturday and had a day free before my meetings
started on Monday. Sunday I rented a car, drove north toward Point Reyes,
and attended the church of John Muir. I walked under the redwoods named
for him and felt as if I had found a home to come to. When I came upon

the trunk of a fallen giant, I stood looking down its broken length in silent awe. The guidebook I'd picked up at the visitors' center told its story:

"The fallen tree here used to be the famous 'walk through' tree, in which school groups often gathered for photographs. The 225-foot tree crashed on December 22, 1971, breaking into four pieces and snapping a second redwood in its path. What killed the six-hundred-year-old tree? A failed root system.

"A redwood has no main taproot. Many small lateral roots extend one hundred feet from its base, intertwining with roots of other trees. For its magnitude, a redwood has a very shallow root system, descending only ten or twelve feet below ground. Shallow roots help the tree use fog condensation dripped from its foliage.

"After years of foot traffic, the soil around the 'walk through' tree had become so densely packed water could not penetrate and the roots died. . . ."

My mood, one moment soaring to joy, plunged as if its wings were wax, and crumbled, a sad wreckage on the forest floor. Adoration like mine—inordinate love—had killed the tree. The rest of my time in Muir woods, I walked gingerly, keeping to the appointed paths, studying the end of too many people, knowing that here was no home for anyone who had eyes to see.

I left Muir woods and wound my way up Mount Tamalpais. The road frightened me. The curves weren't too bad; I'd grown up in the mountains of Pennsylvania. But the drop-offs beside them seemed to call out. I feared the car would answer and veer off into the abyss of its own accord. Consequently, I leaned hard into the mountain, holding the car on the road by the sheer weight of my intention. I gave up watching beyond the few feet ahead I needed to see and did not look out until I'd safely nosed the front bumper against a barrier in the parking lot at the end of the road.

In front of me, far below, the splendor that was San Francisco shone in sunlight.

I got out of the car, relieved to be on my feet, feeling once more in control of my body, and started up the rocky trail to the top of the mountain. That I could name none of the plants bothered me. I was far from home and knew it. I thought of the mountain I was on and its associations with the poets of the San Francisco renaissance, with Gary Snyder and Lew Welch. I remembered the title of Welch's poem *The Song Mt. Tamalpais Sings*, but I couldn't remember the poem, and I wondered, as I puffed toward the summit, what song the mountain might sing to me if I listened. But the wondering itself, my constant self-consciousness, cut me off from the music.

I paused to rest—the cross-country flight had done nothing for my legs—and looked far out over a heavily wooded expanse, the San Francisco water district, a wilderness area, to the Pacific. Somewhere out there was Japan and China, the pull and the appeal palpable there on the mountain as it never was in the east where I'd come from. Around a turn, a gap in the brush opened to reveal the length of Mill Valley and the wealth of California agriculture stretching to the northeast, a promised land flowing with milk and honey.

I reached the summit and stood at the foot of the fire tower, the glass cage of its top cantilevered over my head; the world spread out before me.

For a moment I thought of Moses going "up from the plain of Moab unto the mountain of Nebo, to the top of Pisgah" and being shown all the lands he would not enter. I wondered if he felt sorrow or elation as he lay down knowing the Lord would cover his body and no man would learn where he lay.

Rested, I turned slowly from the city shining in the south to the forest and ocean in the west, and then to the long valley in the northeast. Never before had I stood in one spot from which I could see all the world offers—wilderness, farm, and city. "Which one," I asked myself, "do you want?" The question jarred me. I forgot Pisgah and Moses, the servant of the Lord. I remembered another mountain, a nameless one somewhere in the wilderness near the Jordan River. Two figures stand at its summit. One is Jesus, tired and weak from forty days of fasting. The other is the devil. Scripture says the devil showed Jesus "all the kingdoms of the world in a moment of time."

The view must have been much like the one before me. But the devil didn't ask, "Which one?" He knew no modesty. He waved his hand over it all and said, "Mine." Then, I imagine, he looked shrewdly into the eye of Jesus to see how he understood before recklessly squeezing the universe into a ball and pitching his overwhelming offer, "If thou therefore wilt worship me, all shall be thine."

For an instant, a long timeless moment, on Mount Tam, the world in all its irresistible glory spread before me, the devil's deal seemed a bargain. "Yes!" I wanted to cry out. "Yes! Yes! Give me the paper, I'll sign. I want it. I want it all!"

Then a bird called. And from the distant city the low drone of traffic reached my ear. I saw that fallen redwood, that giant broken into four pieces by the eager, scrambling feet of children, and I wanted to weep. I would not sign. For all the world I would not sign. But as I turned to descend, I felt like Peter remembering the cock's crow; birdsong would never be the same.

the edible yard

FOR YEARS, when my wife wanted me to plant flowers, I'd joke, "The only good yard is an edible yard." My interest was self-interest. I thought only of my appetite, of enough vegetables to last the winter. Into my small plot I crammed snow peas, potatoes, green beans, broccoli, cauliflower, cabbage, zucchini, summer squash, acorn squash, swiss chard, spinach, two or three kinds of lettuce, tomatoes, carrots, beets, cucumbers, turnips, and green peppers. Besides those, I had a blueberry hedge, an asparagus bed, a strawberry patch, rhubarb, a pie cherry, and several apple trees. I planned on being well provisioned. And for a time I was. In fact I grew fat. I swelled from a trim 155 pounds to a prosperous middle-aged 185. I was eating myself to death.

The first thing to go was the strawberry patch. I turned it over. The flaky, delicate crusts of my wife's pies became a memory. Next the rhubarb went. The patch remains, lovely pink poking through the last wet snows, and then luxuriant green burgeoning through the summer, but the red stalks, after one token, ritual spring pie, are given to svelte friends. I gradually cut back on the amounts and the variety I planted, until the last few years I've grown only broccoli, beans, and a salad garden. Last summer, tired of pitting cherries for healthy oatmeal-based cobblers, I yielded the tree to the birds. They came in flocks, and with them came the neighbor's cat, a huge, black and white tom who climbed the tree and lurked sometimes successfully in the branches.

But I did not yield the blueberries. Those I covered with a net draped over tall, white stakes. Daily I turned it back and picked the deep-blue, sugar-charged berries for my morning cereal. Sometimes I simply stood between the bushes browsing, raking the berries into my hands and stuffing myself like a happy bear. One day, however, after I had been away, I returned to the hedge and found the net tangled, collapsed into the bushes. As I loosened it to raise it up, I found a finch head dangling from the mesh. The story was easy to read: The bright berries. The finch. The entangling net. The neighbor's tom.

The last few nights, the temperature has dropped below zero. As I look from my window, I see nothing but the cold of the blowing snow that has rounded the edges of the summer world, making everything but the hot splurges of bright birds at the feeders indistinct and vague. They come for the oil sunflower seeds. Cardinals. Finches. Chickadees. Juncos. Titmice. Mourning doves. Evening grosbeaks. Nuthatches. Even brown cowbirds. And of course, bluejays. Always the brilliant, scolding, impatient bluejays. I love them all.

About the same time the birds were feasting on my cherries last summer, I dug a small pond in the yard, mounding the dirt behind it and rimming it with a low stone wall. I planted bushes around it, spirea and barberry. I planted rushes in the pond and a water lily. Toads immediately took up residence in the wall. And by late summer a leopard frog appeared, floating in the lily pads. Mornings, doves would dawdle down the slanting flat stone into the shallow water to drink and splash.

One creature I had little patience with—the fat groundhog that made its home under the barnwood shed near the asparagus bed. She had a routine I could not thwart. She exited from a hole on the north side of the shed, ducked through the overgrown day lilies into the protection of the waving asparagus, slipped along under the blueberry hedge, plunged through the rhubarb, and entered into the glorious heaven of the broccoli, which she stripped leaf by leaf until nothing but straight, tough stalks remained. I flooded her hole and bricked it up. She emerged from a new exit trailing little groundhog kids. I ripped up the floor of the shed and parked my mower and cart on the dirt. She removed herself to the other side of the garden, tunneled under four cords of maple, and dug a burrow under the garage, where, I expect, she sleeps as I write.

Remembering all this, I am beginning to think of my edible yard as a smorgasbord for creatures other than myself. The finch head in the net haunts me, and I wonder if I can bring myself to share the blueberries. I wonder if I can make peace with the groundhog. What can it cost me? A few berries. Some fencing for the broccoli and beans. "Why not?" I ask myself. From this vantage in the midst of winter, a peaceable kingdom seems a worthy dream.

I don't eat as much as I used to. I'm down to nearly 170, and I think I've learned that "man does not live by bread alone." I think I'll put in a few more blueberries. That way I'll have enough to share and provide, as well, a covered path to the butterfly bush I mean to add to the plantings beside the pond.

My gardening neighbor might not be pleased with my inclusiveness. The groundhog may prove too much for either of our tempers. Even Thoreau lost patience and contemplated throttling and eating a ground-hog raw. I won't go that far, but I understand that parboiled and fried they aren't too bad.

killing the snake,
foiling the birds

THE WATER SNAKE showed up in the garden Sunday morning. I was picking lettuce and heard a soft plop in the lily pond. Delighted, thinking the pond had attracted a frog, I turned to look. The snake lay draped over the lily pads. Three feet long. Thick bodied. Brown with copper markings.

My first reaction was to laugh, "Build a habitat and take what you get." Many summers I'd shared the garden with a visiting black racer and had gotten along fine. Through the afternoon, the snake sunned on the rocks or curled under the silver mound overhanging the water, and I realized I didn't have a visitor. The world I'd made was too inviting—warm water, sunny rocks, shade, and all the fish the snake could eat. I had a resident. My benign, accepting thoughts began to change.

My pond, like the rest of the garden, requires tending. Almost daily I reach into the water to pick off dying lily pads, to wind around my hand the long green algae that seems to bloom at the mere suggestion of sunlight, to adjust the fountain flow, and to clean the blowing detritus of the garden from the surface. I was sure I didn't want to reach into the darker parts of the pond without knowing where friend snake lurked. I was also sure I didn't want to weed around the silver mound without the same knowledge.

I couldn't drive it off with a hoe. My slightest movement toward it caused it to slide off the rocks into the water. I couldn't go after it in the pond for fear of ripping the liner. Early Monday morning I made up my mind. Whatever violence it might require, I would keep my paradise snakeless.

My first plan was simple. I boiled an egg, baited my minnow trap, and submerged it beneath the lily. It quickly filled with sacrificial fish. I counted on the snake's greed to do the rest. I imagined it, hungry, following the fish into the trap, eating its fill, and drowning. All morning the snake, fat, lazy, warm, and imposing, lay in the sun.

Lacking patience, I kept thinking of the neat little .22 rifle with its scope waiting on the shelf in the bedroom closet. With it I can shoot a half-inch group at fifty yards. The snake was as good as dead. But I knew I could not use it. Too many children in the neighborhood. Too much good sound sense in my head. Too little distance between my house and my state trooper neighbor.

I thought of another option. Fifteen minutes after my call, my friend Willis, and his teenage son, Jonathan, arrived with a powerful, quiet pellet rifle. We located the snake under the silver mound. Willis shot at what he thought was the head. The snake disappeared, trailing blood, into the deepest waters of the pond. Five, ten minutes later—it seemed forever, Jonathan pacing back and forth, eager to rake it from the depths—the snake rose to breathe. I sat in the grass, set the crosshairs on its eye, and squeezed. The water exploded, and the snake flipped belly up.

We stood, briefly, looking at the white belly under the water. The wounds from both shots were plain to see, Willis's halfway back the body, mine in the side of the head. We congratulated ourselves on our marksmanship. Then I took the hoe to hook the body out onto the grass for disposal. Lifted into the air, the snake suddenly twisted, writhed, and slid from the hoe back into the pond. Once more we watched.

When it next emerged, it was behind a clump of reeds, slowly raising itself to crawl onto the rocks and to escape into the shrubbery. Not as good at standing shots as Willis, I handed him the rifle. He hit it in the head. Once more we congratulated ourselves as the snake floated belly up in the water. This time I hooked it immediately with a rake and swung it clear of the pond. It was a good thing, for again it twisted and thrashed. But caught on the teeth of the rake, it could not get free, and Jonathan finished it with a slicing shovel blade.

Word of my great snake caper spread quickly among my friends, and I found myself, over the next few days, defending my action. "Had it been a black snake," I said, "I never would have shot it. But water snakes have attitudes. It was spoiling the pond and garden for everyone." Deep inside, I couldn't decide if I felt pleased with myself for asserting my will or guilty. Certainly every time I reach into the pond, I am pleased to be without the snake. But I wonder. Would I be more pleased had I come to terms with the habitat I'd made and the creatures it attracted? As I reflect, I think I determined my action based on the general sense that the garden, however natural it appears, is not wild. It is, in my imagination, a human space, as surely as is my living room. Therein is the problem. Living rooms have walls. Gardens are open to anything that wanders by: groundhogs, snakes, deer, songbirds, and neighborhood cats. Gardens go wild around the edges. They remind us that human spaces exist within a larger space, a wilderness we can't control. They remind us that, while some exercise of control is appropriate to human survival, control is limited. But the reminders they give us about those limits are ambiguous. Might they be merely the limits of our strength, cleverness, and will? Or are they more profound—moral limits which we pass at some peril?

Aesthetics and the size of the pond are what finally shaped my decision; the pond is nine feet long and five feet wide. Out of a desire to create a place I think beautiful, I'd dug it myself, lined it with flexible, black vinyl, and ringed it with stone. It stays healthy because I filter and circulate the water. It supports a population of minnows, darters, and dace because I stock them. It blossoms with lily blossoms because I paid hard cash at a nursery for a lily and winter it carefully in my basement. It is, when all is said and done, a fictive pond, an image of nature made, like any work of art, for human enjoyment.

Were the pond real, larger, say several acres, and surrounded by reeds and cattails rather than Japanese perennials, I'd probably never have seen the snake. And if I had, I would have stepped aside, admired its wild beauty, and recognized that I was in its world. But in the small, cultured world of my garden pond, the snake was out of place.

This clash of culture and nature is constant, though not always so violent. Most often it slips by, an unnoticed encounter, part of the way we live. The same afternoon I shot the snake, I built a framework over the blueberry bushes and enclosed them in a net to foil the hungry birds they attract. Without feeling any ambivalence, I draped that net to protect my berries. As I write, however, the two acts are linked in my mind. What they share is my drive to control the terms of my life. I will not have a water snake spoil the serenity of my garden pond, and I will eat all the fruit I want.

opryland and the ethic
of the garden

OCTOBER RAGES about me. The sumac on the back hill flames red. The maple beside the drive is wild for gold. And against the gray woodshed, the morning glories, touched by frost and dying at their highest stretch of summer, flush lavender and purple.

The garden is finished for the year. A few tomatoes hang pumpkin-orange from withered, straggling vines, but I've pulled the peppers, the broccoli, and the squash. Already the mound they made on the compost pile is settling. And when I look across the yard, the only blossoms left are the deep maroon-reds of the chrysanthemums against the silver of the sage. Still, the garden, however finished it may be for the year, is not done. For the last several weeks, I have been hard at it, thinking ahead, preparing for next year.

I've laid out a fresh design of beds, a design conforming to my waning desire for vegetables and my growing need to be surrounded by flowers, butterflies, and hummingbirds. Where once the garden was flat and thick with beans, potatoes, and lettuce, I've built small rolling hills around a winding path, sprouting grass sown only a week ago. At the beginning of the path, I will pause beside a bed of thyme growing about a sundial. At its end, I will sit on a bench enclosed by white flowering tobacco, purple butterfly bush underplanted with impatiens, and a thicket of spiky, bright bee balm.

My design is good, and so is my intention. But I'm not completely easy in my mind about it all. A few questions, as persistent as dandelions, keep me weeding my assumptions as well as my beds, for while I've been shoving dirt around, I've also been reading and thinking about gardens with a group of students. As a starting point, we've been considering Michael Pollan's *Second Nature,* an exhilarating rip through the world of the gardener and the environmentalist. Beautifully written, funny, and filled with an obvious good sense, it is an easy book to like. It is also a book that, on reflection, becomes increasingly troubling.

Pollan's genius is his ability to see through the smoke of a romantic view of wilderness derived from taking our Thoreau straight-up followed by a chaser of Muir. He is brilliant when he demonstrates the inadequacy of the resulting "hands off" ethic to speak to the niggling, practical problems of everyday living. Having driven a wedge into the grain of the oneness of culture and nature, the ethic's absoluteness becomes its flaw. We are forced into choosing between *either* and *or.* Forced into that box, few Americans, pragmatists that we are, are likely to choose against our own interest. Nature will lose. Recognizing this, Pollan asks, "What if now, instead of to the wilderness, we were to look to the garden for the makings of a new ethic?"

Much of what he offers in answer to his own question is wise and helpful. I liked his book, and I'm pretty sure I would like him. But at least one of his suggestions disturbs me deeply. "'Garden' may sound like a hopelessly anthropocentric concept," he writes, "but it's probably one we can't get past."

Yesterday, turning from talk to action, my students and I traveled the sixty miles or so from Houghton to Canandaigua to spend the afternoon being guided about Sonnenberg Gardens. The nine formal gardens we saw were designed in the early years of this century by Mary Clark Thompson and were planted as a memorial to her husband, City Bank founder Frederick Ferris Thompson. As we followed horticulturalist Ray Sanger from garden to garden, what seemed to be a refrain in his talk, "Of course, they had money to do things we can't," began to impress me. Whenever he used it, he was pointing out future restoration projects, but it stirred questions about the adequacy of Pollan's garden ethic in my mind. Those questions came to blossom near the end of the afternoon as we explored the ninth garden of the day, the rock garden.

We entered it from a path winding along one of the many water gardens, a water garden bone dry because of the long drought of this past summer and the inability of the trust to afford Mrs. Thompson's purchased flood of city water to fill it. The path turned quickly into the side of a hill, and we found ourselves walking at the bottom of a deep crevice lined with puddingstone, a conglomerate chosen for the garden because its natural pitting makes ideal pockets for rock plants. As we stood in the coolness of that path, Ray explained that the whole hill had been created for the garden. Every boulder, every yard of soil had been hauled in and placed by hand. The thought, "Of course, they had money to do things we can't," ran through my mind.

Then, suddenly, the import of it, the troubling part of Pollan's garden ethic, smacked me. I had seen this garden before.

Several years ago, acting only out of duty, I boarded one of the jets of Agony Airlines, allowed myself to be lifted from the security of the earth and hurled southwest from Buffalo to Nashville, where somewhat to my surprise I was landed safely. There I transferred to a courtesy van and was driven through the night to the hotel where I would confer with a great number of other fools on matters of great academic importance—Opryland.

It was shortly after Christmas, and the grounds were lit up like the sequined suit of a country star. Inside, I passed from the bright lights of the check-in desk to the near darkness of the Cascades, the first of two interior gardens designed for the country music lover's pleasure. I could see nothing except the tiny lights reminiscent of those that would have come on in the aisle of the jet to guide me to safety had its "systems" failed. I followed them through a maze of shadowy plants and wound up on what the brochure I purchased at the end of my stay describes as "an elevated walkway that winds through a forty-foot-tall mountain, over cascading waterfalls and under towering palms." It was, I must admit, a gaudy-awful, impressive place. I hated it instantly.

Before finding my room and flopping my suitcase on the stand, I also wandered through the second of the gardens, the two-acre Conservatory,

63

where the emphasis is not on water but on plants. It too was dark and left me with a vague sense of being safely lost but thoroughly disoriented.

The next morning, in search of a bagel, I discovered a "nature walk" wound through the Conservatory. Twisting back on itself, winding over running streams, and climbing sudden quick hills, it was cunningly made. I admired the gardener's tricks. As I walked, I noted the plants—and the signs identifying them: travelers palm (a clever choice), false bird of paradise (a name of almost biblical appropriateness), fiddle leaf fig (for Charlie Daniels), ponytail palm (for more than half the line dancers in the nearby club). I thought of Wallace Stevens's poem "Anecdote of the Jar":

> I placed a jar in Tennessee,
> And round it was, upon a hill.
> It made the slovenly wilderness
> Surround that hill.

Bagel-less, I grew grumpier and grumpier. I needed a jar of my own to place in the middle of the exotic sprawl to give it some order, some reason to be. And that was the trouble. The garden was neither wilderness nor art. It was climate controlled: 71 degrees; humidity between 60 and 65 percent; watered with a sophisticated drip system; flora without fauna—except of course that strange, plastic-toting creature *Touristus Americanus*. It was simply a collection of plants, a display any amount of money could buy. Before I left to return home, I bought my wife a gold-plated oak leaf and promised myself never to return.

But there in the rock garden at Sonnenberg, I realized, I had returned. I stood once more on an artificial mountain with a cascading fall of city water to soothe my soul. I stood in the midst of what money could buy, and then I thought of my own garden, my hand-shaped rolling mounds, my dugout pond with its circulating pump, my tricky hedge that blocks the neighbor's lawn from view and brings the far hillside near. Standing there, I was discouraged; the garden in its every manifestation appeared nothing more than an imposition of the human imagination on the landscape. Then, for the moment, whimsy saved me. I remembered Marianne Moore's description of poems as "imaginary gardens with real toads in them." I would have it that way, the garden as art—with real toads, butterflies, and hummingbirds.

Here at my writing desk, however, whimsy will not do. I return to Pollan's question, "What if now, instead of to the wilderness, we were to look to the garden for the makings of a new ethic?" I fear that that ethic would care little for Pope's advice to "respect the genius of the place." I fear that we would choose to push the earth in mounds to suit our dreams and fence (or roof) them off from the wild, the only truth that gives them life. I fear our ethic, founded on our anthropocentric wishes, lies, and dreams, would differ only in a few details from the developer's we so deplore.

the larger flow

psalms

a prayer
for wholeness

What once was here, O Lord,
I hold in my imagination's eye—
the forest grown to climax,
the elk, the bear, the wolf
at home, a part of your
intention for this place.

Though I cannot by my labor
change for good the way
this valley yields to willfulness,
one man alone
against devouring man,
I give to you the work
that you have given me.

That the constancy
of my labor might be
my unceasing prayer,

that the fragrance
of humus held to my nose
might rise
an acceptable sacrifice,

that my heart and mind
might incline to no profit
other than your joy,

that my work might be,
at last, your work,

bring wholeness to your earth,
the trees I plant
grown to praise the Christ
incarnate in the wood,
the maker of
elk and bear and wolf.

the clever trout

The clever trout that nips
the mayfly from the air
is quick to praise
the maker of his sight.
His speckled side
reflects the light;
he swims as he
was made to swim.

The slender popple
at the meadow's edge
is in the Spirit
also giving praise.
Its lean into the wind,
its supple ways
declare it stands
as it was made to stand.

The raucous jay,
that scolding streak
of blue, gives warning
to the quiet wood.
He knows my nature
is not good.
"Beware," he cries
as he was made to cry.

From these, O Lord,
the creatures of your love's
abundance, let me learn
to forsake
the wild desire that drove
my father Adam to shake
the garden tree and claim
a glory of his own.

Before them, strike
me dumb. Let me see them
as you made them
in delight.
Then give me grace
to praise as well your bright
presence as the trout,
the popple, and the jay.

to Christ
the creator

Praise to you, Creator Son,
for all the creatures
of this earth too small
for any notice but your own.

With your eyes I see
the six-inch snake,
green as mint, soft
as a baby's hand, curled
about my finger,
and love it with your love.

With your eyes I see
the crayfish, hard
as a toenail, brown
as the mud beneath
the water's rippled surface,
and love it with your love.

With your eyes I see
the nuthatch descend
headfirst the maple trunk,
its blue-gray feathers
light against the bark,
and love it with your love.

With your eyes I see
all these and more.
I see the turtle's
painted shell,
the eft's red body
on the crumbling leaves,
the green frog's
leopard spots,
and the snail's bright
trail shining
in the morning sun.

For these I give you thanks,
and for your presence
in their making and unmaking,
I give you praise.

Each small life is yours!
In wonder I meet
the richness of your grace
and love you with your love.

approaching war

All here is quiet,
held fast in the stillness of snow.
Nothing moves.
Even the wind is bedded down.

I alone am restless,
moving about the wood,
bearing my unease
like a weapon.

I am here to lay it down,
to yield my will
to him who speaks the earth
anew each morning.

Yet what I lay down is seized
by powers ready to say the death
of every panicked bird
flushed by shuffled feet.

Who is so angry
he rages against the morning?
What cause has he
to scorn the day?

When will the earth
refuse his need?
Where will he
find rest?

He is angry whose heart
is dark with joyless striving.
His evil rises with the light
and stretches across the day.

Soon the earth will shudder.
A cloud will form above
the desert, and he will find
his rest in fire.

Forgive us, Lord, who
in our yielding stand wordless
in the light.
Our failure is disease.

It grants dominion
to the shuffling powers
whose fire
is the end of speech.

This earth, both wood
and desert, is your holy place.
By grace we dwell in it.
By praise we hold it as your own.

lament

Three springs break from the hillside.
Like the laughter of children
their waters gather
into the single song of Salvation Brook.
Without ceasing, through the longest days
of summer, its clear voice gives
its maker praise.

Beside its hemlock-shadowed pools,
the heart-shaped prints of deer,
mingled with the spoor
of possum, coon, and mouse,
declare such news as people
perish for want of hearing.

Here I would settle into joy,
be found a part of all
that sings such praise.
But I am lost;
the news I hear from distant lands
is news of peoples dying.

In Bosnia: death.
In Israel: death.
In South Africa: death.
In Los Angeles: death.
In Haiti: death.
In Somalia: death.
In Liberia: death.
In Grenada, Panama, and Iraq:
death.

Father of Mercy, who shall be found
innocent? Who shall be found
while Christ incarnate
suffers in the flesh he came to save?

Here where all would be well,
I am found a part of all I would not be.
Here in the presence of your creatures,
I lift my hostage voice
and keen.

a prayer for order

Father of all creatures,
whose dwelling extends beyond this world,
let no one trivialize your being.
Let your order prevail.
Let your intentions come to be
for creation and for yourself.
Give us, each day, no more than we need,
and forgive us when we take for ourselves
the well being of others,
as we forgive others who seek to take ours.
Lead us away from our dreams of power
that we might be whole,
satisfied in you.

my delight

Though you have made the earth
for your delight,
I walk your woods and find
in hemlock, pine, and poplar
shelter
from the burning of your sun
and fuel to warm me
when your cold descends.

I find streaming from the hillside
clean water
that slakes my thirst,
and in the wildness of its flow,
trout that feed my hunger.

At your meadow's edge,
I pluck raspberries from the cane
and wonder at the thrasher
in the briars.

With every turn I find
extravagance—
the unending revelation
of your joy's abundance.
What other end should I imagine
for goldenrod and buttercup,
for bloodroot, trillium, and phlox,
for jack-in-the-pulpit
and Queen Anne's lace, for coltsfoot,
mullein, vetch, and lily,
for loosestrife and forget-me-not?
I am confounded.

What harmony within yourself
led you to make your pleasure
and my needs be one?

What awful purpose then
led you to place
your pleasure in my keeping?

What discord now tempts me
to seize what you have made
and call it mine?

The fitness of this place
for my abode portends
a grace beyond
my strength to hold.

I must be held or fall.

With these words affirming
my delight, I yield
my inclination to name
my own what can be only yours.

Let my delight be as it must
yours and yours alone.

the larger flow

The little spring that breaks
an affirmation from the hill
tumbles one hundred feet
to Salvation Brook,
where it is gathered
into the larger flow.

Salvation Brook sings over stones
and spreads into a tiny marsh
before dropping, lined by popple,
through sloping fields
into Houghton Creek,
where it is gathered
into the larger flow.

Houghton Creek, a springtime
torrent, rumbles through town
carving clay banks and deep pools
where bait fish thrive in safety.
It pours into a lazy bend
of the Genesee,
where it is gathered
into the larger flow.

The Genesee meanders north
through corn and beans,
falls plunging through
the Letchworth Gorge, and quiets
at Mount Morris Dam.
Controlled by engineers,
it plods a dociled beast
to Rochester and cascades into the waters
of Superior, Michigan, Huron,
Erie, and Ontario,
where it is gathered
into the larger flow.

Ontario empties through
a thousand islands
into the Saint Lawrence,
a big water dividing
nation from nation until
it meets the backward push
of the North Atlantic tide,
where it too is gathered
into the larger flow.

All waters then are one.
Let us rejoice: wherever
we are seated listening
to the song the waters make,
we are beside the wholeness
of your sea. And we, there,
seated in our solitude,
are like the waters
being gathered in your grace
into the larger flow
of your unbounded love.

praise

This and only this
is what since childhood
I have wanted:

to stand in a small woods
both strange and friendly,
where fern and skunk
cabbage thrive in hemlock
shadow, where sunlight
mottles the leaf mold
at the meadow's edge.

Once, in the uncertainty
of early adolescence,
I stood, almost worshiping,
in a dark wood.
Frightened by all
I could not name,
savage in my innocence,
I carved a totem
from a stick and left
it standing in the shade.

Now, in middle age, I come
to Remnant Acres. Mystery
surrounds me. But born
into the body of Christ,
I carve no totem. It is his Holy
Spirit moving in the wood
who makes creation new.
Enclosed in grace,
happy to be here,
I stand owned by the end
of all my wants.

When I speak his name,
The wind lifts up my praise.

the garden
of corporate desire

These spendthrift pilgrims
have faces washed with tan.
They have come to worship mammon
and redeem their happiness
from the fires
of corporate earth.
Their eyes miss nothing,
for they have learned the art
of being watchful
as they move across this land
where nothing they could want
is not for sale.

One wheels a stroller piled with goods
and drags a candy-eating child.
One, a plastic badge clipped
to his shining suit, checks his watch
as he weaves slickly
through the crowd. Another,
capped with wild, unruly gray,
shuffles slowly close
to the windows stuffed with manikins
of youth. He holds himself on guard.

Five, boombox-loud in black and silver,
moving like a school against
the sluggish current, nearly knock
him down. In their laughter
he tries to catch himself, settles
beneath a palm and fades away.
Two girls, half-dressed in cutoff
jeans and clever tops, jabber by.
Firm in fifteen years, they do not miss
the shabby stare
of the adolescent clerk in the shoe store
front. They pause, lift a purple
sandal in his gaze,
judge him less than satisfactory,
and flip away.

O Christ! Where in this grim
garden enclosed against the wilderness
of wind, sun, and insect buzz
do you walk telling stories
of seeds and stones and light?
One among these many, no stranger
in this strange land,
I hum a wordless song
and seek your stunning face.
In what flesh do you hide yourself?
Why when I look so wildly in my need
will you not be seen?

The candy-eating child grabs at
his mother's slacks. She heaves
him to her hip and hustles on.
The shining suit breaks stride,
stops, and orders ice cream
from a red-smocked woman
who fails to meet his eye.
Under the palm the old man nods.
The black and silver
five are fish he plies for pleasure
in his dream. And the clerk,
carefully placing the sandal
on its stand, longs to know
the touch of one bright girl,
to find beneath the mocking light
of movie love a truth more formidable
than he has words to know.
The girls flounce out of sight.

But Christ! In the flashing
moment of their presence,
in the child, the suit, the old man,
and the boy, I see,
not hidden, but dwelling where any
quickened to the wildness
of your love might see,
that you are here.

I see your stunning face.

Here in this sheltered garden
where all is priced to sell,
your grace is free.

Be praised, incarnate Christ.
Be praised.

a prayer for grace

Eternal Unchanging,
for pleasure you move the continents
where you please.
Shoving great mountains into folded heights,
you send wind and water
to wear them down
and build deltas of sediment
to hold the record
of your wild love
for making living things.

For joy you swell the oceans,
roll them over the land,
and make shores where water is no more.
For delight you gather them into ice
and send it ranging over mountains and plains,
carving wide valleys,
spreading erratics,
and leaving moraines and till
when you call it back.

Lord of time and change,
creator and destroyer of the gentle,
lumbering brontosaurus
and the swift carnivorous beasts
that preyed upon it,
maker of the mollusk and the worm,
wake us, who tear down mountains
to light our homes,
who slaughter species
with our growing love of deadly things,
who splice genes
and name ourselves gods,
to the image of yourself,
the love that you have placed
in us to call us back
when we would wrest control of change
from your unchanging inclination.

Teach us to ride your grace
as lightly as the mountains
rise and fall
to your voice making each day new.

the valleys have ears

The valleys have ears, O Lord.

The mountains need not roar,
avalanche snow and scree and boulders
down their sides to awaken
sullen glens.

It is enough for mountains to remain
long, though they must change.
Let them be the good news
of your quiet voice
to the spirit-shadowed,
the light, broken groves,
and the wild gardens
stretched beside the streams
of your mercy.

Let lichen and moss break rock.
Let your rain fall justly
on high and low.
Let your living water carry
the new soil, a fertile ground
for the seed of your word,
to meet the surf of your sea.

The valleys have ears, O Lord, and voices.
With every rising shoot of green,
they name your name.

Except for sheer exuberance, O Lord,
the mountains need not roar.
As well as any height,
the valleys sing your praise.

the wild

two gardens

LINDA SAT on the weathered log bench, looking through an opening in the trees. Far below her the Hudson River rolled coolly toward the Atlantic. I stood facing her. Sweat pouring down my back, I itched and fidgeted. The temperature and the humidity were pushing the upper nineties. We were at least a mile from the car. The trail up had been rugged, and I knew descending it would be hard, if not dangerous. Linda urged me to relax, to enjoy the view, but I was so angry with myself I didn't care that Henry Hudson had anchored the *Half Moon* in the waters below. Nor did I care that Ian McHarg had said of the wild garden where we stood, that it "may be the single superb example of ecological design in the United States. If it were in Japan, it would be a national treasure." I was upbraiding myself for having encouraged Linda, rock after rock, up the mountainside, risking hearts and ankles to end up where we no longer wanted to be.

We had come to this mountain perch because I was on sabbatical trying to understand something of the way Americans relate culture to nature. Manitoga, the garden we were exploring, had been at the top of my list of sites to visit. Once a logged mountainside and quarry, the eighty acres just north of New York City had been purchased for a summer retreat by Russel Wright, an industrial designer known for his home furnishings and an aesthetic seeking harmony with nature. Wright spent thirty years restoring the land, creating a *natural* landscape enhanced by a network of trails, carefully placed boulders, native plantings, and designed views of the river called *osios*, before opening the garden to the public in 1975. He said his object in making the garden was "to help people experience the wonder of nature in a new and intensely personal way."

I was doing that as Linda and I rested at Chestnut Oak Ridge Osio, the end of a spur two-tenths of a mile off the main trail. Sitting there, we didn't know that was where we were. Though we had picked up a map at the kiosk in the parking lot, where I had dropped a seven-dollar contribution into the locked metal box, we were lost. Nothing was right. The correspondence between nature and map we trusted did not exist. As I grumbled about the mapmaker, we labored blindly up a trail as rough as some in the Adirondacks, fought deer flies, and saw almost nothing we could not have seen on any hillside back in the Genesee Valley. By the time we reached our lonely bench, I was sure we had left Wright's Eden behind.

I realize, now, that though we had not strayed beyond the physical boundaries of Manitoga, we had, in a very real sense, never entered it. Because we had approached the trailhead, described on our map as a "subtle opening," from a slightly different direction than the mapmaker had anticipated, we had walked right past it and had hiked the trail backward. That alone guaranteed that we would not see the purposeful landscape Wright had designed. But more important, even if we had started out correctly, time had altered Wright's work. The purposeful landscape had been overgrown by a truly natural landscape, and the artful human features had been absorbed into a larger, more obscure, pattern. We walked that morning, despite Wright's intention and McHarg's assertion, not in a garden but in a woods.

An hour or so later, after a garden salad at McDonald's, we pulled into the parking lot of Sunnyside, the nineteenth-century home of Washington Irving. From there we had only a short walk down a wide, curving path to the visitors' center and a guided tour of the house and grounds.

After living in Europe for more than fifteen years, handling family business and serving in diplomatic posts, Irving bought a one-hundred-year-old Dutch cottage in 1835. He also bought the surrounding ten acres, a small fragment of what had been the Manor of Philipsburg. He then set about constructing what he described as a "little nookery somewhat in the

Dutch style." What he built was a bit more complicated than his description suggests. Collaborating with artist George Harvey, he redesigned the cottage, preserving its Dutch character but also incorporating features modeled on Sir Walter Scott's Abbotsford and a tower deriving from the monastic towers he had seen during his years in Spain. As a consequence, the cottage, as small as it is, embodies Irving's sophisticated cultural history.

In designing his gardens, Irving brought other influences to bear. One was a simple pragmatism. He was not a wealthy man, and the economy of country life determined some of his choices. Describing his project in a letter to a friend, he wrote, "Indeed I can live cheaper here than elsewhere, and benefit my 'Kith and Kin' into the bargain." Quite consciously, he created a working farm and incorporated the most modern technologies into it. At the same time, just as Wright would do a hundred years later, he sought to create a *natural* landscape that invited guests to wander along paths and to experience picturesque views of the Hudson. Thoroughly romantic, he wrote, "I think it is an invaluable advantage to be . . . in the neighborhood of . . . a river, a lake, or a mountain. We make a friendship with it, we in a manner ally ourselves to it for life." He demonstrated this friendship by interacting with the landscape. He enhanced the river views by judicious arrangements of both native and exotic plants. And he hid the working gardens, the stables, and the woodpiles behind screens and fences. The effect he created was so successful that Sunnyside became known as America's Home, and images of the house and grounds were featured by Currier and Ives and in popular magazines throughout the nineteenth century. Our tour of the house ended in the enclosed kitchen garden. We crossed it and strolled along a path past the icehouse toward a pasture and orchard. Through the trees and shrubbery to our left, we kept catching views of the Hudson. We retraced our steps and wandered back to the cascading stream and the pond Irving called the Little Mediterranean. A green heron was fishing on the far side of it. We sat on a bench and felt very comfortable.

The guidebook I bought at the visitors' center states that "Sunnyside epitomizes the then-prevalent Romantic movement in architecture and landscape design, expressive of a yearning for an idealized past." No doubt that is true, but I do not think it is nearly the whole truth. The work of restoration, the creation of a new forest, that Russel Wright achieved at Manitoga is exemplary work. The work of living performed at Sunnyside is also exemplary. To the extent that the work at Manitoga attempts to subordinate the human to the rest of nature, it represents a manifestation of our contemporary longing for wilderness. Acting on that longing, however, can be an act of division, a sundering of humanity from nature, a creation of the human as an alien creature. Though I believe in wilderness and would set aside larger tracts than any president has yet dared, fly-bitten and aggravated on the Manitoga mountainside, I felt alien. The mountainside was beautiful. I plan to go back. But as I looked around, I saw no evidence of a living relationship, no evidence of the harmony Wright sought. I saw, instead, a fragmentary peace achieved by the banishment of the human. As a human, I found that problematic. At Sunnyside, among the working gardens and the exotic plants, I participated in Irving's act of friendship. I was, for a moment, at home in the world.

lizards, cardinals,
and steven spielberg

IN HER RECENT collection of essays, *High Tide at Tucson*, Barbara Kingsolver describes her work as a graduate student observing desert lizards. She tells us they don't do much. While her conclusion does not surprise me, her ability to patiently observe interests me. It is an ability worthy of emulation, one that might stand for the wholeness of a fully human participation in the physical world. It is nothing less than the ability to pay attention. Because I treasure this ability, I try to stay away from the movies, and because in my imagination the movies and television are one, I try to avoid television as well. That I have inhaled the impatience of both like secondhand smoke does not change my aversion.

I remember being taken to a Lassie movie by my parents before I reached school age. The film, of course, was in black and white and by the standards of today's movies was pretty tame stuff. One scene, however, remains vivid in my memory. Lassie and an old man are lost in a blizzard. For some reason they must cross a snow-covered log bridging a raging stream. Lassie will not step onto it; the snow is too treacherous. So the old man sits on the log and begins to hunch across it, spilling the snow so Lassie can cross. I assume he was successful, but I don't remember; I was so frightened I hid under my chair and would not come up until the film was over. My father was disgusted, but I didn't have to go to another movie until some years later when *The Robe* lit up the screen in full color. By then I'd seen televi-

103

sion, and I was prepared for excitement. To the embarrassment of my mother, I stood in my chair and yelled encouragement to the hero throughout the action scenes. I still hadn't gotten the message that movies are only movies.

And I still don't. I think they shape a secondary reality that replaces the world. The first night of the Gulf War, I sat in my living room drinking my dessert coffee and watched the bombing of Baghdad. Like every other American, I was transfixed. It looked like a movie. It felt like a movie. It was a movie. But two seats in my Introduction to Literature class had been empty that day because the students they belonged to were huddled in tanks at the border of Kuwait, wondering if they would face biological or chemical agents when their orders to advance came down. That I had to remind myself someone was dying every time I saw one of those neat smart bombs explode like a video game image hurt me as a human being. It made me something less than what I was born to be.

Though the images I have used so far have been images of violence, violence is not my concern. A full and accurate participation in the dailiness of life is. A few days ago, I stood with my morning coffee at the kitchen window and watched a golden-red female cardinal at the feeder. She seemed to be enjoying her morning the way I was enjoying mine, for she sat facing the lawn, leisurely working a seed in her beak until the hull dropped to the ground before turning back for another. She stayed a long time, and I began to time how long it took her to pick up, hull, and devour a single seed— ten to fifteen seconds. She was a dainty eater. But really, she didn't do much. She simply sat like one of Kingsolver's lizards, making me happy to be alive.

I went into the living room and turned on *Good Morning America* for news of a different sort. Paula and Harry were talking to some experts about the future of television. According to them, the screen is going to disappear and I'm going to have a bunch of holograms dancing on my coffee table. Though Paula and Harry oozed enthusiasm, I'm not sure I like the idea. If already I cannot tell the difference between the Gulf War and an action movie, what difficulty will I have with holograms? Imagine how Kingsolver's lizards will come to us in this brave new world. One doesn't have to; one only has to remember *Jurassic Park*. Those lizards did things. That those silly, computer-generated beasts were designed not to enlighten or make us care for the world but to titillate our fears and remake the world into a place of facile horror doesn't seem to matter. They are exciting.

The world, however, doesn't need to be remade. It certainly doesn't need to be made into a realm of pointless horror. It needs to be engaged and loved. I do not doubt new technologies will come. I am confident the distortion of reality caused by seeing the world only through them will continue. It will continue because much more appears to happen on the screen than in the world, and we are suckers for action. But I'm not interested in having my senses so overwhelmed that the world becomes boring. I love the world as it is. Consequently, I plan to continue staying home from the movies. I intend, as much as possible, to avoid television. And most important, I plan to use the time saved to stand at the window, to walk in the woods, and to watch cardinals and lizards do just about nothing.

a sandbox in the sun

I MUST HAVE BEEN nine or ten when the alligator arrived in the mail. It wasn't addressed to me. It was addressed to my little brother. And it probably wasn't an alligator. It was probably a caiman, a smaller, more docile creature better suited to the tourist trade. Still it was shipped from Florida, from the Everglades, from that great grass river of alligators, water moccasins, panthers, and birds of such exotic feathers one could imagine a swirling flight of color brighter than a prairie sunset. I knew, even then, that someday I would go there.

We were on the back patio about to eat lunch when the box arrived. My brother, a five- or six-year-old budding herpetologist, received the package eagerly. He set his grilled cheese and tomato soup aside, tore the box open, and reached in to claim his prize. It bit him.

The small damage it did to his finger paled beside the damage it did to his psyche. He howled. My mother leapt from her seat and ran for the antiseptic. I proved myself useful by plopping the shipping box over the enraged critter and stepping aside. Appreciating my quick action, my mother declared, "It can stay there till your father comes home." My brother, frightened and wounded underneath his returning bluster, was content to wait for reinforcements.

Alligators, I've recently learned, are more interesting creatures than we commonly assume. The female alligator, contrary to a somewhat hardened exterior, is a gently maternal beast. She watches over her nest of eggs. She helps open the shells when the newborns begin to emerge. And she gathers the little ones in her mouth and carefully carries them to the water, where she bears them on her back for safety.

So maligned by writers—even Audubon feared the gator's night-long bellowing, and Muir wished him an occasional "mouthful of terror-stricken man by way of dainty!"—the alligator has survived through eons by a combination of unexpected qualities. First, its brain is no larger than an acorn, a pretty small portion of smarts to govern a body that grows from the moment of birth to the moment of death. As a result, it stays focused and entertains no extraneous thoughts, no self doubts. Watching one sink silently, disappearing into the dark of water, a human viewer recognizes a presence to be reckoned with. Second, the alligator possesses tremendous strength because of its ability to tolerate huge doses of adrenaline. This strength lasts through short bursts of activity. Third, the alligator weakens quickly. To compensate for this, nature has made it master of the art of doing almost nothing. Capable of reducing its heart rate to a few beats a minute, the alligator can lie underwater with its mouth open and wait for food to trip its jaws, which close faster than the human eye can follow. Equipped with a sophisticated mechanism for controlling its body temperature, it will lie partially submerged, shifting slightly, altering the amount of skin exposed until it finds comfort.

Confined under a box on a stone patio warming in full sunlight, my brother's alligator, a near infant that should have been riding its mother's back in some tepid backwater, suffered a hopeless ordeal. When, near sundown, my father lifted the carton, he found a shriveled carcass.

Last fall in the late daze of October, having breakfast at an outdoor cafe in Palm Beach, I thought of that story and laughed. It returned to me strangely as a pleasant memory of a fifties childhood, a story connected to dyed Easter chicks and foul-smelling, half-dollar-sized turtles sold at the five and dime. The memory passed, and I sat welcoming the ocean breeze softening the humid heat my thick northern blood could not thin fast enough to enjoy. Yet as I sat there, so coddled in luxury's lap, I began to feel out of place. I was in Florida to lecture, to give a poetry reading, and

107

to fulfill that lifelong dream of visiting the Everglades, but nothing looked right. I grew increasingly uncomfortable, grumpy, and unsettled.

My companions, transplanted northerners, confessed to me that in spite of the way they kidded their friends in Minnesota and Wisconsin, they missed the changing seasons. I took their confession as an opportunity to blurt out, "Palm trees must be about the ugliest things God ever made."

My friends looked at me as if I had lost my mind.

"What amazes me," I continued, trying to explain what, in fact, I had lost, "is how clever God was to arrange them in straight lines and space them so evenly."

Just then a flatbed tractor-trailer loaded with half a dozen horizontal palms pulled around a corner.

"God at work," one of my companions said.

The other smiled and launched a utilitarian defense of the silly palm. "Many of the palms you'll see south of here were punched in after Hurricane Andrew. Where the oaks go down, the palms bend and survive the winds."

"I can see that," I said, "but they're still ugly."

This demonstration of my pathological lack of appreciation of cultural and biological diversity would be typical of my whole time in Florida. Though I wanted to like it, something held me back. At first I thought it was merely my northern cold-climate chauvinism, but as the days passed, I began to understand; it was the straight lines, the punched-in palms and all they stood for.

The Everglades have their source in the waters of Lake Okeechobee. The Florida Peninsula, a recent geologic phenomena, stands only sixteen feet above sea level at the lake surface. It drops roughly one inch per mile from there to the Florida Bay. The waters, the great grass river of the Glades, creep southward to the Keys at the rate of one mile per day, a current barely visible to the watchful eye. It is a fertile place, fecund and frightening to the accounting mind. After reading about it before making my journey, I suggested to a friend that its productivity reminded me of how power should be distributed in a democracy—wide and shallow. My friend replied, "That may be appealing to an anarchist poet, but if anything's going to get done, somebody has to get in there, channel it, and make it work." Trusting he was joking, I laughed.

My trip into the Everglades was a modest, one-afternoon excursion. Rather than going into the Everglades National Park along the Tamani Trail, my friends and I traveled Route 84, the famous Alligator Alley, west from Fort Lauderdale and turned north onto a quiet two-lane built up through grasslands and cattle farms that led to Big Cypress Seminole Indian Reservation. As I traveled along Alligator Alley, I watched the canal dividing the road from the wide expanse of grass. Bass fishermen maneuvered their boats from spot to spot, casting for thrills and trophies. Anhingas, like avian martyrs, hung themselves from low bushes, drying their wings. Only after egrets became so common that I began to ignore them did I see my first alligator, loglike and motionless, floating in the dull canal beside the highway. The sudden frisson I'd expected never came. The primitive rush of wildness I longed to know was absent, impossible in the ordinariness of automobile travel and the atmosphere of weekend recreational activities around me.

Though we had been in the Everglades most of my drive, I had no sense of being in them until I climbed onto a swamp buggy, a four-wheel-drive vehicle resembling a beached pontoon boat, took a seat behind the guide, and was carried into the river beyond the circle of buildings that served as a gathering for tourists like myself. Even then, as the buggy crawled through the shallow current creaking and heaving under and around the water oaks, swamp maples, and sable palms, I never shook free of my long van ride over the interstates. I never escaped a sense of myself as a tourist wandering through a cleverly designed theme park.

I kept a notebook open on my lap, writing illegibly as the guide lectured. At one point, we stopped to watch young, chocolate fallow deer, an introduced exotic, jousting. Their antlers tangled; they used their seemingly fragile necks to lever each other halfheartedly back and forth in preparation for future, more earnest conflicts. A little later we watched feral pigs rooting about, oblivious to our intrusion. As I examine my notes now, I am able to make out only the names of a few plants and the list of birds I recorded: great

109

white egret, white morph of the great blue heron, ibis, curlew, night heron, red-shouldered hawk, sharp-shinned hawk, cattle egret, belted kingfisher, boat-tailed grackle, and vultures.

What remains most with me is the character of my guide. A grizzled son of a missionary, he kept answering questions by proclaiming, "It's the way it is because God wanted it that way." At one point, he stopped the buggy, turned, and loosed a near prophetic word, a burst of scorching sarcasm at what humanity was making of God's intentions. "Look around," he said. "This place wasn't made to live in. It was made to absorb storms and hurricanes, to filter water and be a nesting place for birds. It was made for alligators and snakes. People come, channel the river, scrape what dries up clear to the sand, punch in palms, then cry to the government for aid when what any fool knows is going to happen happens." He paused for his words to register. Then with rueful grin added, "And the government, of course, pays."

I thought, *There's a story in the Bible about that* and caught his eye. I didn't need to speak. His expression told me he knew the same stories I did. He jammed the buggy in gear and as we lurched forward, he spoke over his shoulder. It may have been to everyone; it may have been to me alone. "When you're driving back to Fort Lauderdale, take a good look at Weston."

Several hours later, back on Route 84, the sun at my back, I looked from north to south. To the north an expanse of grassland stretched farther than I could see. Under it the water flowed. To the south, a few inches lower, Weston, or what was being added to Weston, was spreading over a naked, white sandbox. It was as if a child had taken his hand and leveled the surface, dug a system of canals, drawn straight lines for roads, set up houses, and stuck twigs for trees in the yards before them. I looked north and shuddered, for as I looked to the grass, I knew what I turned my back to was every bit as vulnerable to destruction as the sandbox world of the child. The guide was no fool. *Where, around here,* I wondered, *is there a rock to hold to?* For all my need, I could not see one.

I returned to mocking the palm trees. It seemed safer and more polite than anything else I might say. And I thought about the gators waiting in the canals.

Then I felt the frisson I'd missed.

The wild was all about me. Hidden in the false front of punched-in palms and highways made straight through the wilderness, it waited for the day when the canals would overflow and the river of grass would inexorably spread, taking back what rightfully belonged to it. Time, I realized, was on its side. And the gators, its most potent manifestation, having perfected the art of doing nothing, could wait as well. *The sandbox in the sun*, I thought to myself, *does not belong to anyone; it belongs to itself and to the God who made it the way it is because he wanted it that way.*

When my father lifted the box from my brother's alligator and called us to come see what had happened, we did not mourn. We did not know what we had lost. My brother took the carcass and buried it as deeply as he could dig under his sandbox. Some months later he dug it up and carried the skull into the house. Without intending to, he loosed it in my imagination, where it lurks, its heart rate reduced to a few beats a minute, its mouth open, doing everything the wild must do to human dreams.

rose pogonias

AMONG PEOPLE WHO CARE about such things, the word is circulating: the rose pogonias are out at Moss Lake. Several years ago, as a reward for two hard days of work rebuilding the boardwalk over the floating mat for visitors to the preserve, Betty Cook, botanist and Nature Conservancy board member, led me out onto the moss for a close look at the tiny orchids. When the news reached me that they were out, my memory failed me; I couldn't recall a visual image. To correct that failure, I set out to visit the lake.

The orchids were supposed to be growing in two places—far out on the mat where Betty had shown them to me and halfway around the lake close to shore. My arrival at the small parking lot of the kettle lake discouraged me. Six or seven cars and vans filled it. Multiplying by an average of four people to a vehicle, I guessed nearly thirty people besides myself would be crowding the narrow trail. I backed out of the lot, parked on the road outside the preserve, and walked in.

A family of too many noisy children occupied the little clearing on the shore opposite the parking lot and picnic table. They were watching a pair of mallards swimming at the edge of the mat and a Canada goose cruising the open water. Had they come two years ago, they would have been feeding the swarm of stunted brown bullheads that turned the calm lake into a cauldron of boiling flesh the instant a crust of bread hit the water. Once when my daughter was a child, I held a quarter-slice of cracked wheat two inches from the surface. The fish leapt and tore it from my hand. I held

another piece at the edge of the water and scooped up a fish that flopped onto shore to take it. I offered it to my daughter, but she preferred sight to touch. Another time we watched a three-foot water snake twist through the frenzy and slither off beneath the bog cranberry. But there are few catfish now. A winter ago, too many fish competing for too little oxygen led to a population crash.

Across the lake, I could see a slew of people on the boardwalk, so I turned aside from the trail and climbed onto a smooth, gray log protruding out over a small, lily-filled lagoon. As I settled with my arms propped on my knees to hold my binoculars steady, a large wake moved through the water about twenty yards away. My first reaction was surprise. The wake looked like one made by a swimming beaver. But that made no sense. I raised my glasses. A huge snapping turtle—its shell must have been eighteen inches across—floated just beneath the surface of the water. Slowly it extended its primordial, beaked head onto a lily and hung suspended in the water. For what must have been five minutes, living in a different world, I sat equally motionless, watching, before it silently sank from sight and disappeared.

I lowered my glasses and looked around. On a distant log four dark bumps looked interesting. Through the glasses, I saw they were painted turtles. I scanned the far shore of the lagoon and found two more hauled up on the mat. A quick look over the lily pads revealed two others. Those did not stay in sight long. The ones on the log proved the most fun to watch. They seemed to get themselves balanced on the log and then forget where they were. They'd flail their legs in the air without touching the log surface that curved away from them. Then, it seemed accidentally, they'd extend a claw and at last touch the log. Reoriented, they'd raise themselves and move a few hesitant steps along it or slip without sound back into the water.

I sat quietly enough that one eventually crawled onto a log almost directly beneath me. I don't think he saw me—how well does a turtle see?—but he never settled in the way the distant ones did. Cars kept coming and going behind me, and I wondered if he could sense vibrations. Perhaps he simply heard the noises of the eager nature consumers and was agitated, for at a sudden door slam, he pitched forward and plunged nosefirst from the log.

Agitated, a nature consumer myself, I swung down from the log and started out the trail to find the rose pogonias I'd come to see. As I walked, I thought about the turtles and tried to find the right word to describe the red stripes on their necks. *Red slashes* seemed close, but I rejected it as too violent, too much of the observer in the observation.

The rumored cluster of orchids near the shore I never found. I settled for a long view from the boardwalk of the group I'd seen close up with Betty Cook. I suppose I should have been disappointed. They were almost invisible to the naked eye. Even through the glasses, they showed only as small splotches of rose-purple against the mat. The intricate detail that makes them so elegant remained beyond vision. But I really didn't mind. Just knowing they were there, spread out with plenty of room between them, satisfied whatever need I was feeling.

I walked to the end of the boardwalk and looked across the lake to the parking lot. It was empty.

I was alone.

I looked into the water. No catfish swarmed at my feet, but I was sure they were there, a small number of them, scorning the wonder bread of humanity, growing large and healthy the way they were meant to grow.

appalachian autumn:
three mountains

1. the knob

I'M DRIVING a borrowed car. It has 179,000 miles on it, no fifth gear, and my destination is the highest knob on the Virginia–West Virginia border. With every wild curve, I question my sanity. But on this road, in these mountains, who needs fifth gear? The houses I pass, though they are well kept, have an air of tenuousness. They lie close to each other, cuddled up on the narrow level spots between the road and the stream on one side or the sharply rising mountain on the other. Threatened by both water and stone, they appear very American, accidentally placed, eager to be somewhere else.

The road winds upward. It is October. The leaves are at their peak of color, but this year, I'm told, has been dry; they are dull rust. Still, I am absorbed in them, finning upwards like a diver seeking the surface, seeking the light and the good air above me. They are all I see.

Then suddenly, I am above the rolling surf of the trees, driving through scrub. Miles of autumn plunge away. The road narrows to a single lane, and I shift from third to second to round a switchback. Over the dash, I see only sky. I hug the shore of leaves. I shift into third for the short straightaway, then back to second for another brush with the void, and I am at the top.

I am 4,383 feet above sea level. In the Adirondacks, I've climbed lower mountains and felt good. Here I feel strange. To the south I see only mountains. If I weren't standing beside a backhoe perched against a pile of gravel, I could imagine myself in wilderness, but I am, I cannot forget, in the George Washington National Forest. I have driven a car to this vantage.

I turn west. Cleared fields sprawl along the ridges before me; a few of them hold barns. Though I can pick out neither cattle nor sheep, sunlight glints from windshields of cars and trucks abandoned to rest at the ends of the dirt lanes twisting up from the occupied intervals. Still looking west, I settle on a field of satellite dishes. All facing the same direction, all aimed at the same spot in the sky, they do not comfort me. They sprout, not like the fruit of Eden, but like great white fungi. They are the satellites of our naval communications system. They are the crop of that Jeffersonian gardener, West Virginia's own Senator Byrd. What messages they receive and send have no eloquence fit to preserve any good thing I love.

I cross the parking lot, stand on the stone wall, and look north. It looks like the west. I want to feel good. I want to feel some sense of awe at the expanse. I want to feel in my bones the age of this place, the depth of the ancient sea, the unimaginable heave of the upthrust, and the long wearing down that made Ohio and the plains beyond my vision. But I feel nothing. I am simply one figure among others on the top of a mountain, looking out at the mundane everyday of the end of the twentieth century.

This feeling is underlined by my companions on the knob, a college student, probably a freshman, and his family—mother, father, little sister, and dog. Their car has a New Jersey license plate, and they joke about the absence of hills at home. Carrying bottles of water, they roam about, pointedly ignoring me, talking about life below. They climb to the top of the gravel pile, calling the dog to follow. Manfully, on short legs, dragging its belly, it labors in response, slipping badly at each heave upward. Finally it stands at their feet. Sliding back down, they laugh at themselves and at the hapless dog. Plopped on the pavement, they pull off their shoes and empty them. They have reached a great height, and they have no words to meet it.

When they depart, I move to the east and watch their car appear and disappear on the switchbacks below me. Then I take my binoculars from their case and look back to the small city where I began my morning journey. I find the grain mill at the center of the town. Poultry is big. The economy is turkey. A haze is settling over the valley. I long for a bottle of water.

I walk once more around the parking lot. Pausing beside the backhoe, I entertain monkey-wrenching thoughts. What business has a machine in the wilderness? If I knew how to start it, I could put it in gear and aim it over the side. How beautiful it would look tumbling down, turning over and over, coming to rest upside down, out of commission, useless and forlorn. How beautiful it would be if it would tumble all the way to the satellite garden. But the thoughts are nonsense. Not only am I afraid of taking such an action, I am too much a respecter of state property. I like the road I drove up here. I'm too old and broken down myself to haul my carcass this far from home without a mechanical aid. I like what troubles me.

So I go down, carefully in second gear around the steepest switchbacks, then in third. Only when I am well down the mountain do I shift into fourth.

2. lift up my eyes

I PULL into a parking lot across from a small sign showing a striding figure with a walking stick. I get out and look up. The overhanging trees prevent my sight from reaching the mountaintops, but I know the tops are up there; I could see them from the valley as I drove west to get here. Deep in a narrow interval, standing between the car and a dry creek, I examine my shoes. They are relatively new, comfortable, but not made for hiking. I cross the road, bound over the shallow ditch at its side, and step onto the trail. It's rough. Sharp rocks protrude from the ground, roots twist over it, and it is steep, slicing up the mountainside at a forty-five-degree angle to the road. My shoes are all wrong. A hundred yards will shred them. I start up anyway.

After only a few steps, I know to go slow. I'm five hundred miles from home, and I've told no one where I am or what I'm doing. I don't know where I am. Not exactly. Somewhere on a nameless mountain somewhere in western Virginia. Other than up, I have no idea where the trail leads. Today, that's enough. I have no other direction I want to go.

Quickly I'm winded, and I rest. I've been watching only where my feet go, and it is good to look around. The trailhead is out of sight. The road is out of sight. Ahead, I see a long, rising line scored into the side of the mountain. Leaf-covered rocks punctuate it like a sentence written by a comma-crazy schoolmarm. *When in doubt, leave it out,* I think to myself. Out loud I say a line from William Stafford, "I place my feet with care in such a world."

I go on. Upward. Placing my feet with care. The trail appears to end a few yards ahead of me. It is a switchback, and now I am heading along among the tops of the trees whose roots I stumbled over minutes before. Yesterday, when I spoke at an academic symposium, I was introduced first as an environmentalist and then as a woodsman. The moderator paused and said sheepishly, "I suppose that means he cuts down trees." She was right. I partially heat my home with wood. I know the trees of my wood-lot, but here I am unsure. I recognize the maple and the oak. But there are others, many I do not know. Ignorance is bliss.

From far above me I hear a croaking or scraping that suggests a painful bark. I do not recognize the sound. I climb on. What I don't know can't hurt me. Something answers it.

Another switchback. Another rest. This one longer, sitting on a good rock. A pileated woodpecker chortles from below me. Then I hear it knocking. I ask for breath, get up, and go on. I think the shards of rock punishing my shoes, bruising my feet, are granite. But I'm not sure. I ask myself why I can't remember my college geology. A hooting voice in me answers, *Because you took it thirty-five years ago, you idiot.* No excuse. Smart people remember things longer than that. And smart people don't start up trails they don't know in mountains they can't name.

My heart is pounding. No problem. I took my blood pressure medicine. The world is good. More trees. More rocks. Another rest. Another switchback. And I come out onto an exposed outcrop of rock, a ledge with a view. Assuming the mountain I'm on is about the same height as the one across from me, I'm maybe halfway to the summit. I step forward to look down. Three feet from the edge, I stop. I can feel the wind rising. A part of me starts to spin, and I imagine myself caught in the updraft, sailing like a bird. Close enough, I say. I turn back, find a natural seat on the side of a boulder, and sit.

I'm hungry. And thirsty. Very thirsty. Mostly thirsty, and I have no water. Leaving the car, I never gave water a thought. I sit and meditate on water. And bread and cheese. What I need is a good miracle. Muir lived on bread in the wilderness. And water. I remember another wilderness mystic, Jesus, refusing to turn stones into bread. For him a miracle was a simple temptation to please himself. He did without bread. When it came to water, he did without it also. He told the woman at the well about living water and never thirsting again. I could use about a quart.

Moses also did a little wilderness travel and mountain hiking. His solution to the water problem appeals to me. I get up, find a big stick, a staff, raise it over my head, twirl it around warming up, and give the rock I was sitting on a good whack. The end of the stick snaps off, flies over the edge, and crashes down the mountain. No water.

I sit back down on the rock. Actually, I sit in the rock, in a sling-backed depression that holds me and allows me to rest without fear of the precipice so close to the trail. Slowly I quiet. The wind blows, bringing an Aeolian music to the morning. A voice, mine, recites over it, "I will lift up mine eyes unto the hills. From whence cometh my help? My help cometh from the Lord, who made the heavens and the earth." In my rock chair, I don't have to lift up my eyes; my eyes are in the hills. That question, though, "From whence cometh my help?" has a context. During the rule of David, the hills were shrines to pagan gods. Looking to the hills was looking up to them. David's psalm redirects us. Our help is beyond the hills in the life of the Creator.

Something about this rock holding me, however, is firm and comforting. It cannot be overlooked. If God is not the rock, he is in the rock, and the rock is a way to him. Jesus said so. He said if humans cease to speak, the stones will cry out.

I listen. Voices reach me from the campground near my car. They are the voices of children at play. A dog barks. Pileated woodpeckers call back and forth. That strange, scraping bark sounds again from above me. This time I recognize it. Hen turkeys, feasting on acorns, are announcing their satisfaction with the world. A car crushes down the road, grinding the gravel under its wheels.

But I cannot hear the stones. The voice of the rock is still.

I go down. My knees hurt, and when I reach the car, I must rest, come back to myself before I am sure enough to engage the clutch and risk a return to the conversation of friends.

3. the stones cry out

IT IS LATE afternoon. I am deep in a Virginia mountain. In the longest-operating tour cave in the United States, I am walking with strangers, listening to a young woman in a green uniform spin a mix of geology, myth, and history into a quintessential tourist experience. Here Thomas Jefferson, George Washington, and John Madison walked together looking in wonder on the candlelit formations Jefferson would later extol in *Notes on Virginia*. Up the ridge, in another cave, they left their names in candle smoke on the stone. Their names can still be read, but not by you or me. That cave is closed. Nevertheless, I am glad to know, under this mountain, that I plant my feet in their footsteps.

I've been here before, not in this cave but in others like it. When I was a child, my mother and father, taking pity on my carsickness, interrupted their leaf-watching along the Skyline Drive and stopped at every cavern along the way. The order of my day is nostalgia. I am here to remember. What I'm here to remember, I think I've forgotten. Perhaps I never knew it. But I'm sure it has something to do with the mountains, the heights I scaled this morning, with light and dark, and the voice of the earth.

This cave, like the caves of that childhood trip, is limestone, filled with columns, stalactites and stalagmites. Here also are shields, strange, gravity-defying formations no one understands. They hang above my head, protrude at eye level, and rise from near the floor. Some weigh half a ton. All glow in the curious light of commercial wonder. Sight is not enough. I want to reach out and touch their shining surface, to feel if it is as smooth as it looks, to know if it is slippery, if it is wet. But I have been warned, and warned again, not to touch.

The cave is a living thing. Human oils left on the stone prevent the flow of water. Because this ends the growth of the formations we have paid dearly to see, touching is against the law and carries a two-thousand-dollar fine. Though our guide seems more impressed with the fine than with the actual consequences of the offense, she has repeated with annoying regularity the mantra "Touching the stone will kill the cave."

My stomach knots as I grasp, once again, how fragile this world is. At the same time, the idea of the cave as a living, growing thing, as a part of creation still being born, excites me. Unable to trust myself, I stuff my hands deep into my pockets and listen, more open than I ever imagined I could be, to the canned speech of this young woman. At any moment, I hope, her words will rise to splendor, will connect with her subject and change forever the way we understand our place in creation.

The caves I know best are the sandstone caves of Pennsylvania. As a teenager, I clamped a carbide lamp onto a ball cap and descended ropes into their gritty depths. I followed the carbon arrows deposited on the rocks by previous explorers and crawled on my belly, hunching myself forward with my elbows through low tunnels to find my way to large open rooms where currents of air bent my lamp flame dangerously back on itself. There was little to see in those caves. Water etched them slowly deeper, but it left behind no formations to backlight and name the Bridal Veil, Bacon and Eggs, or Dante's Inferno. Human oils posed no danger there. In those caves, rock was rock. The attraction was the cool damp, the hardness of the stone against one's soft body, and the dark.

This afternoon, though darkness is behind me and before me, I walk in a surrounding light. The cave, which has had many names and owners, was wired in 1889. At every stop, our engaging doyenne throws a switch, lighting what lies ahead, voiding what lies behind. But her words have not taken flight. Only the present is present, and we stand together, strangers without direction. "Thy word is a lamp unto my feet," the psalmist wrote. Here, beneath the mountain, we have lights, but no light. What we have heard is the *no-word*, the vain repetition of false worship, the complacent vanity of a people stuffed with the good lies of their prosperity.

At one stop, a five-thousand-square-foot space called the Grand Ballroom, our guide tells us how dances were held on its leveled floor in the early nineteenth century. Unchaperoned young women would stand with a hand on the "hitching post," a dead, waist-high stalagmite at one end of the room, to indicate their willingness to dance. After dancing, so many couples wandered into the dark of a more dangerous willingness, that the owner, fearing for his reputation, brought the dances to an end.

No dancers among us, we stand in a long hall—our guide calls it a room. Far down it, a single stalagmite rises from the floor. Its shape is obvious, primitive, phallic. She asks us to guess how large it is. A knowing crowd, we can spot a trick when we see one coming. No one speaks. She sends a ten-year-old boy ahead of us to stand by it. As he walks away, he grows small. Beside the stone phallus, he is tiny, diminished, negligible. We titter, pretending to laugh at our distorted perspective in the vastness of the hall. We think of the "hitching post," and I wonder if the lesson of the boy's journey has been maliciously planned or if it is just an accident, one of those Freud has convinced us carries meaning.

She calls the boy back. He returns to life size. But her toying with us is only beginning. "Is anyone here afraid of the dark?" she asks.

"How dark?" someone answers.

"Dark dark," she says. "So dark you can't see your hand touching your nose."

"I can see in the dark," a small child brags.

"Not in this dark," she warns. "If no one minds," she goes on, "I'm going to turn the lights out."

"For how long?" a voice questions from behind me.

"About fifteen seconds."

Not long enough, I think. I'm remembering sitting on a cold lump of sandstone at the bottom of Delaney's Cave when I was thirteen years old. I'm remembering taking the lamp from my hat, holding it in my hand and slowly turning down the flame until only an iris of light showed in the center of the reflector. I'm remembering grasping a flashlight in my other hand and blowing out the flame. I'm remembering the darkness slamming into my eyes like a fist. I wanted to see stars. But there was nothing. Absolute, wonderful nothing.

"I'll turn the light out now," she says. I hear the clunk of the transformer in the distance. Suddenly, the light is gone. But it is not dark. Before throwing the switch, she had lit a candle. She is holding it above her head and speaking, "This is how Jefferson would have seen when he came here." A tiny circle of light too weak to reach the walls hangs in the air. As she lowers the candle, a baby whimpers. A flash of darkness strikes our eyes. The baby screams, and the light is back.

Not long enough, I think.

As the group moves down the long room, I stand still, watching the individuals in it diminish as they near the stone shaft. The lights go out behind me and I turn to the darkness.

Standing there, ignoring the speech bouncing from stone to stone, I want one thing: I want to see that darkness as I saw it that day so many years ago in Delaney's Cave. I want to feel it holding me, to know the rising panic of blindness.

And I want something more, something I just remember, something I've been seeking all day: I want to hear the stone crying out, voicing the groaning of creation, the longing we all know for the day of redemption.

But I cannot stay where I am. I must join the strangers in their small nimbus of safety.

I go down the rock hall, pass the towering stalagmite, and stand at the edge of the group. As the cheerful guide begins another playful speech, pointing out a circus of animals to a spellbound child, I step behind a leaning slab of stone. Above my head in the dim light, I follow a line of mineral deposits around the room. It is a waterline. A lake once filled these depths. I breath deeply and swallow, relieving the pressure I suddenly feel in my ears. I am a diver who has gone too deep. And then, for an instant— I cannot be sure—I hear the stones. But they do not speak to me. They sing, a low thrumming like the sound of a top spinning on a wooden table. It is, I'm sure, a kind of praise.

Then all is quiet. "Is everybody here?" the guide questions. I step back into the room. It may have been only the sound of my blood racing.

letchworth:
the genesee at flood

FRIDAY MORNING the river had dropped about three feet from its Thursday crest, which had closed the road. After my appointments with my students, Willis and I drove over to Letchworth to see the falls. The drive down the valley was strangely, eerily beautiful, for on each side of us an absolutely straight line divided the higher, cold air of the ridges from the milder air of the valley floor. Above the line, every tree sparkled with ice. Below it, every tree shone glossy wet. When the road climbed partway up the ridge, we would drive into a different world. As we passed close, we saw that individual trees were divided, half-frozen, half-dripping.

I've seen the river at the spring runoff many times, but I'd never seen anything like what roared through the park. The long, flat water that flows over the slablike layers of sandstone between the upper and middle falls was unrecognizable. How many levels of water plunged and beat against each other from shore to shore I could not tell. Though I could discern a pattern of changes, the changes were too complex to order. A six- or seven-foot fin of water would rise from the current, roll across it toward the far shore, break, and disappear only to be followed moments later by its twin. At two points the whole river doubled back on itself, creating ten-foot-high standing waves that never broke, that simply opposed the rush and announced the form of the rock fifteen to twenty feet below.

Euphoric, I left Willis, who was trying to take photographs and wishing for a different lens, and climbed the trail to the top of the upper falls. I stood as close to the edge as I could without leaving the trail that widens into a walled overlook at the brink. For a moment I thought of the similar vantage one has at the Horseshoe Falls at Niagara. But the comparison would not hold. Niagara is too large to comprehend. Its very scale diminishes one's response. The Genesee, however, is a small river.

I looked upstream to the point where the water pushed upward as it entered the narrow gap spanned by the railroad trestle. It was unmarked by any disturbance, a ten-foot-high wall of greenish-brown water dividing around the concrete bridge abutments. Then it exploded as it widened for the rush to the falls. The two currents rolled over each other, caught a cataract falling from the gorge wall, threw it across itself, battered the stone where I stood, and plunged into the coffee-foam mist that hid the pool at its foot.

I know I was talking out loud the whole time. I was ecstatic, but I could not hear what I said. I do not know what I said.

But I do know this. The smallness of the Genesee is what made it large. The contrast between what I thought I knew and the revelation of what the river is filled me with awe. I think the words I uttered were words of praise. And I do not think they were directed to what I saw. But I do not know. I could not hear. I did not have an interpreter.

Then as I looked straight down—the water seemed to actually undercut the overlook beneath my feet—I saw at the very edge of the falls a flat shelf of rock about eighteen inches square.

Quickly I looked about.

The descent to it would be easy. Trees lined the way; I could hold on to them if the bank were a slippery slope. Thoughts of John Muir far out on the ledge at Yosemite flooded over me. He wrote how he was possessed, protected from danger by the trance of his fascination and wonder. But my trance was not as deep as his. I saw Willis below me and in my imagination Linda at home worried. She hadn't wanted me to come at all. I went down the trail.

There will always be a flat rock at the edge to tempt us to get near. Some will yield. Others will not. But one yielding had better pray for a rope about the ankle and for friends to hold its end. Even the high priest cannot be sure of a return from the holy of holies.

moonwatching with thoreau and basho

twelve proses

(composed in the spirit of haiku)

moonwatching
with thoreau and basho

LATE ONE NOVEMBER evening, I stood on the bridge over Cold Creek and looked downstream to the small gravel delta where its waters merge with the Genesee River. Early snow lined the banks of both the stream and the river and covered the heaps of gravel rising from the dark, rippling water.

Above Snyder Hill, the moon swam through long clouds. Caught in the motion of cloud shadow crossing patches of snow, the landscape shifted unreally. Water, earth, and moonlight became one thing.

Earlier in the evening I had been reading Basho's *Narrow Road to a Far Province*. Standing there, I imagined myself seated before a small hut, moonwatching, and vowed to write a poem about the night, but I did not.

Now, in the depths of another snowy night, I sit near the woodstove and reading find these summer lines in Thoreau: "I saw a distant river by moonlight making no noise, yet flowing as by day—still to the sea, like melted silver reflecting the moonlight—far away it lay encircling the earth. . . . There is a certain glory attends on water by night. By it the heavens are related to the earth."

> Like snow, moonlight
> covers the sleeping earth.
> I watch for dawn.

wanting to be known

THE WIND HAS SWEPT the snow from the corn-stubble ridge and piled it in drifts along the fence. In the woods the snow is deep. I have been walking for hours and have seen nothing to make into a tale to carry home. Hemlocks and beech. White pines and oaks. A few hickories and maples. A single crow cawing and a chickadee flitting silently from bush to bush.

In twilight I stand motionless, leaning on my stick, exposed at the edge of the field. One hundred yards away, seven deer browse the stubble. Delicately aware, they know they are not alone. One in particular looks for me, lowering her head to browse, then suddenly raising it, trying to catch a movement to name.

The stillness in me steps forward. "Here. Here," I cry.

> Whom do I seek,
> wandering in the winter cold?
> One who must find me.

wings

LATE ONE MORNING in March, I hiked the trail up Devil's Back to the ridge above the Genesee River. Though the sun was bright, it was not yet warm. The trail was frozen, and I walked without breaking the thick, white skin covering the frequent puddles.

Wind brushed softly through the oak leaves on the woods floor. Frozen, lifting and falling, they rustled like stray footsteps.

I walked, watching far ahead of me through the trees for tawny shadows. I saw none. But near me, close to the lifting leaves, a small fluttering settled into stillness. The woods ordered themselves about it. A butterfly, rust wings outlined by a double band of yellow and black, lay coolly on a log. As if to begin a prayer, I stepped close and bent down.

> Like a hand opening
> and closing, the wings
> signed in the light.

hawk and heron

THE LEAVES WERE not yet on the trees, though they showed pale buds in the sun. Linda and I were sitting in Letchworth Park drinking coffee where we could watch the river. The falls were upstream, out of sight and out of hearing. Through the trees I watched a red-tailed hawk and several vultures drift in lazy loops, riding the bright air over the river. The coffee in my metal cup warmed my hands.

Linda said, "Look."

A great blue heron was flapping up the river. Directly in front of us it made a wide circle and caught the updraft the silent birds had ridden out of sight. It spiraled upward. Had it not been for its long, trailing legs, I would have forgotten its name. Higher and higher it soared, growing smaller and smaller to my naked eye until, invisible, it filled my imagination.

> Who could do this thing?
> The dead heron at the edge
> of the Spring-stirred pond.

monument mountain

TWO PATHS LEAD up Monument Mountain. One is long and easy; the other short and steep. Both are narrow. Pilgrims intent on following the journey Melville and Hawthorne made the evening they first met, we took the shorter path. It bent away from the parking lot beside the highway and turned sharply uphill. Feet had cut into the mountainside and worn it smooth. We followed easily until we reached a jumble of large boulders. There the path grew faint, and we lost our way. We worked along the base of a cliff, trying every shadow strung between the broken slabs. None went anywhere.

Tired, knowing we had erred, we returned to the mountain's foot. Our path was not the path. Finding the way, we started anew and raced around the boulders. Near the top, we grasped roots to pull ourselves up the final granite staircase.

On the peak, we stood in the wind and looked up and down the highway-split valley. Below, cars spun silently by.

> These journeys we make—
> soundings in the green sea
> of remembered dreams!

fishing for stripers

THE LIGHTS of my brother's truck barely penetrated the storm-dark night as we followed the scrub-lined road through the dunes. At a small kiosk, lighted like a candle, we stopped. The ranger, recognizing a familiar face, waved us through.

We drove another mile to an empty turnout and parked. As we unloaded, the surging Atlantic drowned out the banging of our rods and bait bucket against the truck. Pointing into the darkness, my brother spoke, "Sometimes moose browse the thick brush. Should one turn up, get off the trail."

He splashed a puddle of light on the path ahead of me. "Turn it off," I said. I walked easier without it, keeping my way by the feel of the sand under my feet.

The beach, a lesser dark, opened before us. Far off, beyond the breakers, lightning scrawled the slow progress of the storm.

> Moose browse and lightning—
> what calm the night-fishers know.
> The old world finished.

in the garden

THE POND IS black, invisible, except for the small rippling where the little fall pours its temporal song into the water.

The foxgloves have hidden themselves in pockets of darkness. The blues and reds of the bright verbenas and dianthus have joined the night. Even the white larkspurs have withdrawn and become pale, vanishing shadows against the enclosing hedge.

Only the solar lamp, the soft afterimage of the day's brilliance, reveals its place in the garden's order.

I sit watching. The lamp glows. Fireflies sparkle.

There.

And there.

And there.

I catch their brightness only as it fades.

Beyond their display, the stars, motionless in their eternal motion, shine. I catch their brightness only as it fades.

Morning is far away and near.

> What light!
> The fireflies!
> The stars!

near power

LAST NIGHT in my rented room at the edge of Washington, D.C., I slept only one hour before waking. Lying wide-eyed, I thought of my long drive south along the Susquehanna River through some of the most beautiful mountains of Pennsylvania.

Penn's Woods. The name alone invokes a dream of the peaceable kingdom, where the lion lies down with the lamb. The whole way, I was blind. At sixty-five miles an hour, I saw only furious asphalt and unfortunate spatters of roadkill.

Sealed in my room, I listened to the constant growl of the beltway traffic. Periodically I heard bullfrogs in the ditch outside my window. "Still here," they burped through the night. At dawn I heard a cardinal. Or was it a mockingbird being a cardinal for my ear?

> Hey frogs! What news
> from the narrow ditch? What word
> croaks this beltway morning?

claybed road

EVERY REGION HAS an identifying landmark. When that landmark is something as large as a mountain, a canyon, or a river gorge, the landmark is often known worldwide. Other landmarks are local, of no consequence, known only to a few and shown to visitors with as much embarrassment as pride.

Such a landmark grows off Claybed Road, a short drive from my home. I delight in displaying it to children and to adults lacking humor. Showing it always begins with the leading question, "Would you like to see a pineapple tree?" Even the smallest children scoff, "Pineapples don't grow on trees."

I simply point to the apple-laden tree in the pasture and wait. Rising from the leaves, a scraggly white pine, rooted in soil collected in the apple's crotch, tilts rakishly in the wind.

> The cows
> beneath it graze
> uncaring.

finding the path

THOMAS MERTON had been dead nine years when I went to Kentucky to find him. I was thirty-four and had casually thought of myself as his student since discovering his poetry fourteen years before. The time had come, I'd decided, to know him profoundly.

I thought I might find him in his letters gathered at Bellermine College. I thought I might find him in the liturgy at Our Lady of Gethsemani. I thought I might find him roaming the knobs beyond the monastery walls. Though I learned to read his hand, though I was stunned in silence, though I became lost in the woods and wandered until I stood at the foot of a concrete cross, he remained hidden from me.

I have now lived a life longer than his. This morning, alone in rural New York, reading his journal *Dancing in the Waters of Life*, I suddenly saw the path from his hermitage and knew at once the end of his long silence.

> Under the sickle
> moon, the harvest song of love—
> an old monk prays psalms.

waking to winter

I WOKE EARLY, rose, and went to the window. The lowest branches of the larch, not yet golden with autumn, dragged, snow laden, on the ground. The highest branches drooped, narrowing the spread of the tree. The empty feeder between the window and the tree displayed a three-inch crest of white.

How early this first snow, I thought and moved, dressed, and went out into it.

The air was not harsh. The walks, in fact, had held enough heat from the fall sun that the snow had melted on them, and they stretched, a dark, inviting way into the morning. I walked into town. One light after another appeared in second-story windows as I silently passed through the village center and on to its far edge. There I turned back and began retracing my steps. The second-story lights were now out, replaced by the fluorescent glow of kitchen windows. I imagined the slow gurgle of coffee-makers and the sharp aroma filling the indoor morning.

On the bridge over Cold Creek, I stopped. The banks were white. The dark line of the creek ran freely to the far darkness of the river. There was no moon. The town, just waking to winter, would soon know what I was learning.

> Near dawn, the heavy
> snow-filled sky. The dark chatter
> of water and rock.

approaching the narrows

RECENT TELEVISION news shows have run film of a pod of killer whales swimming within sight of Seattle. What remains so alive in us that we willingly interrupt our consumption of the ritualized stories of violence, economic intrigue, and political scandal to watch spellbound? Could it be that we have not lost our instinct for grace, that, at heart, we desire the salvation of being at home in a peaceable kingdom ruled by laws we cannot divine?

Last summer, aboard *Pneuma*, my daughter's sailboat home, I cruised the waters those whales swim. I was never alone. My daughter and her husband moved about the boat, handling lines, serving food and drink. My wife and I sat back and learned the touch of wind, the light of sun reflecting from the water.

An eagle flew above us. Seals swam, their round heads bobbing, about us. And a sea lion lounged on a distant buoy.

Far to the north the glistening snow of Baker merged with the Cascade clouds, and to the south fiery Rainier stood in mysterious clarity as we silently approached the Narrows.

> The sockeye sky,
> the algae sound. Between the two,
> the Spirit's wake.

acknowledgments

The prologue appeared in *Climb High, Climb Far*, edited by Greg and Suzanne Wolfe (New York: Simon and Schuster, 1996). Used by permission.

All of the essays in "Out Walking" appeared in the *Wellsville Daily Reporter*.

Of the essays in "The Edible Yard," "Of Humans and Turtles" appeared in *The Wesleyan Advocate*, "The Edible Yard" appeared in OE, and "Killing the Snake, Foiling the Birds" appeared in *The Mars Hill Review*.

Of the psalms in "The Larger Flow," "A Prayer for Wholeness," "The Clever Trout," and "To Christ the Creator" appeared in *Standing Ground*, (Grand Rapids: Zondervan, 1991). "The Garden of Corporate Desire" and "A Prayer for Grace" appeared in *Cornerstone*.

Of the essays in "The Wild," "Two Gardens" appeared in *Melieu*, "Lizards, Cardinals, and Steven Spielberg" appeared in *Inklings*, and "A Sandbox in the Sun" appeared in *Radix*.

John Leax is professor of English and poet-in-residence at Houghton College, Houghton, New York. He holds a B.A. from Houghton College and an M.A. from Johns Hopkins University. His work has been widely published in periodicals and anthologies. He is the author of eight books, including *Standing Ground: A Personal Story of Faith and Environmentalism*, *Grace Is Where I Live: Writing as a Christian Vocation*, a novel, and three collections of poetry.

Leax lives with his wife, Linda, in Fillmore, New York. He is an avid gardener and is caretaker of Remnant Acres, his five-acre woodlot.